STUDIES IN THE APOCALYPSE

Printed by
MORRISON & GIBB LIMITED

FOR

T. & T CLARK, EDINBURGH.

LONDON: SIMPKIN, MARSHALL, HAMILTON, KENT, AND CO. LIMITED.
NEW YORK: CHARLES SCRIBNERS' SONS.

STUDIES
IN THE APOCALYPSE

BEING LECTURES DELIVERED BEFORE THE
UNIVERSITY OF LONDON

BY

R. H. CHARLES, D.Litt., D.D.

CANON OF WESTMINSTER
FELLOW OF MERTON COLLEGE, OXFORD
FELLOW OF THE BRITISH ACADEMY

EDINBURGH: T. & T. CLARK, 38 GEORGE STREET
1913

TO

THE RIGHT REVEREND BISHOP RYLE
C.V.O., D.D.
HON. FELLOW OF KING'S COLLEGE, AND
HON. FELLOW OF QUEENS' COLLEGE, CAMBRIDGE

DEAN OF WESTMINSTER

PREFACE

THE University of London instituted last year two short courses of " Lectures in Advanced Theology," to be given by a foreign and a home scholar respectively.

The present writer was chosen to be the first of the home scholars.

The lectures, which were four in all, and were delivered in May this year, have been slightly expanded, and, with a view to the better arrangement of the material, been divided into five chapters. Their original form as lectures has, notwithstanding some disadvantages, been retained.

The first two chapters make no claim to originality. They are simply a very short history of the interpretation of the Apocalypse from the earliest times.

An attempt is made by the omission of details to show so far as possible the real advances in interpretation that were made in

the growing centuries. Since, however, greater
contributions have in this respect been made
within the last forty years than in all past
exegesis, larger space has of necessity been
devoted to this period.

Also, for the convenience of the reader, an
Appendix has been added, in which the critical
analyses of the chief scholars of the Apocalypse
are given.

To furnish such details in lectures would have
been impossible.

The real contribution of the present work, so
far as it is a contribution, is to be found in the
last three chapters.   In these the author has
set forth some of the conclusions which he has
arrived at in the course of a prolonged study of
the Apocalypse and the literature to which it
belongs.   That these conclusions are in the
main valid he is fully convinced, though in
detail they may require occasionally drastic
revision.   Apart from these he holds that much
of the Apocalypse must remain a sealed book.

R. H. CHARLES.

4 Little Cloisters,
    Westminster Abbey

CONTENTS

STUDIES IN THE APOCALYPSE.

CHAPTER I.

HISTORY OF THE INTERPRETATION OF THE APOCALYPSE.

BEFORE we enter on a detailed study of the various methods of interpretation that have been applied to the Apocalypse since the earliest times to the present, I must preface our investigations with a few introductory remarks.

First of all, while recognising the close affinities with Jewish Apocalyptic in general, I must point out one important characteristic that differentiates Christian Apocalyptic literature of the first century of the Christian era from Jewish Apocalyptic.

In the second place, I shall put forward some general and for the most part obvious considerations, which will serve in some measure to provide a preliminary canon of criticism, by the use of which we shall be able to

recognise amongst the many conflicting and
contradictory methods, those methods which
were more or less justifiable from the outset.

Now as regards the first point, while we
must unreservedly acknowledge that the New
Testament Apocalypse[1] cannot be understood
apart from Jewish Apocalyptic, we must also
recognise the fact that while Jewish Apocalyptic
was pseudepigraphic from 350 or 300 B.C.
down to mediæval times, (Christian Apocalyptic
in the first century threw off the cloak of
pseudonymity and the Christian seer came
forward in his own person.) For the full explanation of this change, I must refer the
students of this literature to the second edition
of my *Eschatology* (pp. 173–206). I may
here, however, summarise in a few words the
conclusions arrived at there. From the times
of Ezra onwards the Law made steady progress
towards a position of supremacy in Judaism,
till at the close of the third century B.C., or
early in the second, it came to be regarded,
not as the highest expression of the religious
consciousness of a particular age, but as the
full and final utterance of the mind of God—
adequate, infallible, and valid for all eternity.

---

[1] Sometimes the Apocalypse is called the New Testament
Apocalypse in the following pages by way of contrast to
Jewish Apocalyptic.

When the Law thus came to be regarded as all-sufficient for time and eternity, alike as an intellectual creed, a liturgical system, and a practical guide in ethics and religion, there was practically no room left for new light or interpretation or for any further disclosure of God's will—in short, there was no room for the true prophet, but only for the moralist, the casuist, and the preacher. Henceforth in Judaism, when a man felt himself charged with a real message from God to his day and generation, he was compelled, if he wished his message to be received, to resort to pseudonymity, and to issue the Divine commands with which he was entrusted under the name of some ancient worthy in Israel.

But with the advent of Christianity all this was changed. The Law was dethroned from the position of supremacy which it had usurped, and reduced to its rightful status as a schoolmaster to bring men to Christ, while prophecy was restored to the first place, and prophet and seer were once more enabled to fling aside for the time the guise of pseudonymity and come forward in their own persons to make known the counsel of God.

Hence there is no *a priori* ground for regarding Revelation as a pseudepigraph. It is the work of the Christian seer or prophet John.

Our next task is to furnish ourselves with a provisional canon of criticism by means of which we shall be able to recognise the right method or methods of interpretation as they arise in this historical inquiry.

The New Testament Apocalypse cannot be understood apart from Jewish Apocalyptic literature. Like other books of this literature, and, indeed, like most of the prophetic literature in earlier times, it appeared at a time when fear and despair were at their height. Whatever use such books made of past events, their main lesson was addressed to their own age. Now the date of the New Testament Apocalypse belongs unquestionably to the latter half, or rather to the close of the first century A.D.

The writer, therefore, is addressing his contemporaries towards the close of the first century. We have now to inquire : Do the visions of the writer relate to contemporary events and to future events as arising out of these ? that is, are we to interpret the book according to the Contemporary - Historical Method ? Or are we to explain the book as referring wholly to the future, to definite events in the coming centuries and millenniums that is, are we to interpret the book wholly and strictly by the Eschatological

Method? Now I think we can have no hesi-
tation in accepting provisionally the former
method in reference to the chief part of the
book. The analogy of the chief Jewish
Apocalypse is in favour of such a decision.
Moreover, the words of the writer himself
support it; for in i. 1, xxii. 6, he states that
the revelation relates to " the things which
must shortly come to pass " (ἃ δεῖ γενέσθαι ἐν
τάχει), and again in i. 3, xxii. 10, he declares
that " the time is at hand " (ὁ καιρὸς ἐγγύς).

The writer, too, is no ancient worthy, but a
Christian prophet addressing his contemporaries.
But it is well to observe that, even according
to the Contemporary-Historical Method, there
remains a certain prophetic or eschatological
element in the book, which arises out of and
yet is inexplicable from the events of the
present. The writer was no mere mechanical
apocalyptist. He claimed to be and wrote as
a prophet, though he was hampered in some
measure by a body of apocalyptic tradition,
which possessed in his eyes an undoubted sanctity, but which required to be interpreted afresh.

We shall therefore provisionally accept the
Contemporary-Historical Method, and in a minor
degree the Eschatological, as the methods used
naturally and unconsciously by the readers of the
book when it was first published. Once more,

the book, like other apocalypses, is to be interpreted with reference to concrete events, and
not to be treated as an allegory,[1] or a spiritual
or symbolical representation of the world's
history. As in Daniel, Enoch, 2 Baruch
and 4 Ezra, definite kingdoms and persons
are referred to, or definite traditional expectations respecting eschatological events or
persons, so also in the New Testament Apocalypse. Thus the Millennium in chap. xx.
is a definite period introduced by the first
resurrection. There were analogous expectations in contemporary and earlier Judaism.
In fact, this temporary kingdom is just as
concrete an expectation as the Messianic
kingdom of which it is a one-sided development. In like manner a knowledge of Jewish
Apocalyptic forbids us to spiritualise or
weaken into a mere symbol the dreaded
figure of the Antichrist. The Antichrist was
identified at different periods with different
historical personalities — in Daniel with
Antiochus Epiphanes, in the Ascension of
Isaiah and the Sibyllines with Nero. That
a like identification is to be found in the
Apocalypse we shall see later. On these and
like grounds, therefore, we shall look askance
on any method which proposes to remove the

[1] Certain portions are of the allegorical type.

references to or expectations of definite events from the book and to reduce it to a merely allegorical description of the strife of good and evil.

But Jewish Apocalypses call for other methods in addition to the Contemporary-Historical and Eschatological with a view to their fuller interpretation. These are the Philological, the Literary-Critical, the Traditional-Historical and the Religious-Historical. In the sequel we shall find that the difficulties of the New Testament Apocalypse cannot be resolved, unless by the application of these supplementary methods. We are, however, anticipating, and it will be best to adjourn the consideration of these latter methods till we deal with the actual periods when they were first applied to the interpretation of the Apocalypse.

Let us now address ourselves to the subject immediately before us, and describe under definite headings the methods of the successive schools of interpretation.

§ 1. *First, then, we have the Eschatological Method and traces of the Contemporary-Historical, with the beginnings of a Spiritualising Method and the rise of the Recapitulation Theory.*

Unhappily no work survives giving us the view of the earliest readers of the Apocalypse.

Quite sixty years pass before we find any
references to it, and over a hundred before any
writer deals at length with its expectations.
Thus, since the real historical horizon of the
book was lost, and its historical allusions had
become unintelligible for the most part, the
use of the Contemporary-Historical, unless in
isolated passages, had become practically
impossible.   On the other hand, the true
interpretation of the eschatological sections,
relating as they do not to the present but to
the coming ages, was still preserved in tradition,
as we shall presently see.

The earliest expounders of the Apocalypse
whose works have come down to us are Justin
Martyr (*ob.* 163), Irenæus (*ob.* 202), Hippolytus, and Victorinus.   In these writers we
find, as we should *a priori* expect, fragmentary survivals of true methods of interpretation.
Thus Justin, who comments on the Apocalypse
in only a single passage (*Dial. cum Tryph.*
§ 81), adduces it in justification of Chiliasm,
or the doctrine of the Millennium, the literal
reign of Christ on earth for 1000 years.   Justin
declares that this is the view of all orthodox
Christians (ὀρθογνώμονες . . . Χριστιανοί, § 80).
The same view is held by Tertullian (*Adv.
Marc.* iii. 24), as it had been earlier by
Cerinthus and Papias.   The first writer who

treats more fully of the Apocalypse is Irenæus
(*Adv. Hær.* iv. and v.). A survey of the passages
in his works dealing with the Apocalypse shows
that the historical relations of the Apocalypse
to its time had almost wholly passed from
remembrance. His interpretation is a mixture
of the literal and allegorical methods. Thus
he allegorises the number 666, yet he protests
against any attempt to allegorise Chiliastic
prophecies (v. 35. 1). The allegorical elements
show that the influence of the Alexandrian
school was at work, which was later systemat-
ised in the spiritualising method of Tyconius.
Yet genuine elements of the Antichrist tradition
are preserved, and Irenæus also is, as has been
stated, a true Chiliast, and takes the 1000
years of blessedness in a literal sense. As the
world was created in six days, and as one day
with the Lord was as 1000 years, the world
would last 6000 years; and, as a day of rest
followed on the six days of work, so there
would follow 1000 years of rest on the 6000
years of the earth's history. After this
temporary kingdom the final judgment would
follow and the new heaven and the new earth.

Next comes Hippolytus, the pupil of Irenæus,
who in several details follows in the footsteps
of his master. Unfortunately his *Commentary
on the Apocalypse* is lost, and accordingly we

have to collect his views from such of his writings as have come down to us. These are especially rich in references to the Antichrist legend. In this connection he takes the two witnesses of chap. xi. to be Enoch and Elijah, and the Antichrist to be from the tribe of Dan.

Traces also of the Contemporary-Historical Method still persist. Thus he interprets the first half of chap. xiii. of the Roman Empire. But Hippolytus does not keep to these earlier and justifiable methods. He, too, has been infected with the Alexandrian spirit. Thus he allegorises the number 666 like Irenæus, and even such a definite historical reference as that in xvii. 10. Here in the words, "They are seven kings; the five are fallen, the one is, the other is not yet come," the Roman Emperors are unquestionably referred to. But Hippolytus makes them symbolise seven world periods of 1000 years each, and determines thereby the time of the Antichrist. Again the woman in chap. xii. is the Church, which is constantly bearing true sons of God—an interpretation which drives most others from the field.

We now come to the most scientific and original representative of this type of interpreters, i.e. Victorinus of Pettau in Pannonia. We class him along with Irenæus and Hippolytus, since like them he was a Chiliast, and still preserved elements of the true and ancient interpretation of the Apocalypse according to the Contemporary-Historical Method. Thus Nero *redivivus* is the first Beast, and the False Prophet is the second. But his most important contribution historically is his theory of Recapitulation. This is, that the Apocalypse does not represent a strict succession of events following chronologically upon one another, but under each successive series of seven seals, seven trumpets, seven bowls the same events are dealt with.

§ 2. *Spiritualising Method emanating from Alexandria.*

From these founders of the true school of interpretation we must now turn to the Alexandrians, who, under the influence of Hellenism and the traditional allegorical school of interpretation which came to a head in Philo, rejected the literal sense of the Apocalypse, and attached to it a spiritual significance only. This theory dominates many schools of exegetes down to the present day. Thus Clement saw in the four and twenty elders a symbol of the equality of Jew and Gentile within the Church, and in the tails of the locusts the destructive influences of immoral teachers. Origen as well as his opponent Methodius rejects as Jewish the

literal interpretation of chap. xx. and in the
hands of his followers the entire historical
contents of the Apocalypse were lost sight of,
the meaning assigned to the text became
wholly arbitrary, and each man found in it
what each man wished to find.

It is no real cause for regret that with the
exception of Œcumenius, Andreas and Arethas,
the Commentaries of the Greek Church on the
Apocalypse have perished. Of these, Andreas
believes with Origen in the threefold sense of
the Scriptures, and finds the main worth of
the book in its spiritual meaning. On the
other hand, he shows his dependence on Irenæus
and Hippolytus, where their interpretation is
historical and not allegorical.

§ 3. *Spiritualising Method combined within
Recapitulation Theory.*

But we must now return to the close of
the fourth century, to Tyconius, the Donatist,
who combines the Spiritualising Method of
the Alexandrians with the Recapitulation
Method of Victorinus. The works of Tyconius
put an end to *Chiliasm* and a realistic eschatology in the Latin Church for many centuries.
The Apocalypse, according to this writer, de-
picted the strife of the Donatistic Church
with the false State Church and the world

powers. The two witnesses were the two
Testaments, the Beast a symbol of the
World power, and the Millennium the period
between the first and second advents of Christ.
The second advent was to take place 3½ days,
that is, 350 years, after the Crucifixion—therefore about 380 A.D.

The successors of Tyconius removed his
references to contemporary events, and thus
originated a purely *abstract* spiritualising
method of interpretation. Amongst these the
earliest and chiefest were Jerome and Augustin.
The latter is more truly a disciple of Tyconius ;
for Jerome stands at the point of transition
between the Realistic and Spiritualising
Methods. Sometimes he adheres to the one,
sometimes to the other. On the interpretation
of chap. xx., however, he is a confessed spiritu-
aliser : " Let us," he declares, " have done with
this fable of 1000 years." Augustin popularised this interpretation of Tyconius, and thus
for the next 800 years the Millennium became
simply an era in the Church's history. The
ready adoption of this view is intelligible from
the new attitude towards the State introduced
by Constantine's establishing Christianity as
the State Religion.

Other members of this school were Prim-
asius, Cassiodorus, Apringius, Bede, Ambrose,

Ansbertus, Beatus, Haymo, Walafried Strabo,
Berengaudus and others.   Most of these were
untrue in a greater or less degree to the
method of their master, as they introduced
into their exegesis elements of realistic eschatology from Irenæus and Victorinus.

The usual interpretation assigned to the
1000 years' reign of Christ, namely, that it
signified the era of the Church History beginning either with the birth or Crucifixion of
Christ, aroused in the eleventh century, especially in France, the greatest alarm.   The hour
of Antichrist was at hand, and the end of the
world.   Multitudes of men gave or bequeathed
their possessions to the Church, a religious
revival sprang up, monasteries were reformed
and Churches filled with ardent worshippers.
This movement reached its height about the
year 1000 and then died away, to be revived
as the 1000th year from our Lord's Crucifixion
drew near, only again to die away.

When we come to the twelfth century the
Church has wholly overcome its dread of
Antichrist and a closely impending end of the
world.   Secure in its sovereignty over the
world, it believed that it realised in itself every
expectation that the apostolic community had
looked for from the Return of Christ.   Ignor-
ing the darker side of the apocalyptic forecasts,

it surrendered itself more and more to the secularising tendencies of the time, and became self-complacent and corrupt.

But this secularising tendency in high places gave birth to a strong reaction in the other direction in certain communities within the Church. Protests from without were to be found on every side among the various heretical sects which, according to William of Newland, were at this time as numerous as the sand of the sea in France, Spain, Italy and Germany. But it is not these that now concern us, but those that arose from within the Church. The internal corruption of the Church and its growing secularisation called forth anew the apocalyptic temper, which found utterance in Norbert and still more in Hildegard, but reached its highest expression in Joachim, Abbot of Floris in Calabria.

§ 4. *The next school of interpretation, therefore, represents a combination of the Eschatological Method involving Chiliasm with the Recapitulation Method and borrowings from the School of Tyconius.*

Joachim [1] (1195) finds the Apocalypse to be a book consisting of eight parts—a history of

---

[1] Since we owe to Joachim of Floris a very notable *Commentary on the Apocalypse*, and since, moreover, it is one of

the world from its beginning to its close.   He
divides it into three world periods, the first,
that of the Law or of the Father, namely, the
Petrine period ; the second, that of the Gospel
or of the Sons, namely, the Pauline period,
which according to his reckoning was to come
to a close about 1260 ; and the third, that of
perfect liberty or of the Spirit, namely, the
Johannine period.

The duration of the first and second periods

the most important works that have been written on the
Apocalypse, not intrinsically but from the standpoint of
history, I propose to give here some of the few facts which we
know about him.

He is said to have been born in 1145 in Cälicum, a village in
Calabria.   At the age of 14 he went to the Sicilian court,
and some years later made a pilgrimage to the Holy Land.

On his return he became a monk in Calabria, and at the
age of 33 or thereabouts, Abbot of the Cistercian Monastery
of Corace.   Joachim was a deep student of the Bible, and his
knowledge was so profound, for his time, that it was attributed
to miraculous illumination.   Joachim himself maintained
that he was not a prophet in the essential sense of the word,
but that the spirit of understanding had been given him, and
of insight into the prophetic contents of the O.T. and N.T., so
that he gathered therefrom the course of the world's history and
the changing fortunes of the Church.   He recounts (*Comm. in
Apoc.*, p. 39), how one Easter night, while he meditated, the
entire contents and meaning of the Apocalypse and the Concord of the O.T. and N.T. became clear to him suddenly by a
divine revelation.   The three Popes, Lucius III. (1181), Urban III.
(1185) and Clement III. (1187), encouraged Joachim to publish
the disclosures made known to him by God, and to submit his
writings to the judgment of the Holy See.   Thereupon Joachim
resigned the Abbacy of the Cistercian Monastery, and betook

amounted to 6000 years, or six world ages, in harmony with the six days of Creation; then followed the seventh, or the Sabbath rest, of 1000 years, being part of the third period.

But, again, the second period, or that of the Son, falls into six periods of work and strife on the part of the Kingdom of God in the world, and these six times of work are represented in the first six parts of the book. The seventh part contains the Sabbath rest, and

---

himself in 1192 to a solitary mountain region in the neighbourhood of Cosenza, to the great indignation of the Cistercians, who used every effort, and even appealed to the Pope, to make him return; but in vain.

Joachim, with the approval of Celestine III., established a new Monastery in 1196 in Floris, and became its Abbot. About this time he wrote his *Commentary on the Apocalypse*. In 1200, two years before he died, he states, in reference to his three chief works—the *Concordia, the Expositio in Apocalypsin*, the *Psalterium decem Chordarum*, and smaller writings—that the first had been submitted to the judgment of the Holy See, and that he wished all the rest to be similarly submitted, in case of his death.

This statement is all the more remarkable, seeing that about this date it was a current saying that, when Richard, King of England, and his bishops had come to consult him, he had made to them the astounding disclosure that the papal chair would presently be occupied by an antichrist, whom St. Paul had described as a man of sin and all ungodliness, and that he was already born.

On Joachim's death the Cistercians did their best to have him officially condemned by the Pope, but Honorius III. published a decree to the effect that Joachim was recognised as a true Catholic by the Papacy. (See Döllinger, *Der Weissagungsglaube und das Prophetenthum in dem Christentum*, 319 sqq.)

the eighth the consummation of all things. Moreover, each of the first six parts has again its six times of work and its relative Sabbath rest.

But the contents of the six parts of the Apocalypse he states more definitely as follows : the first treats of the priests, the second of the martyrs, the third of the doctors of the Church, the fourth of the monks and virgins, the fifth of the Church in general, and the sixth of the judgment of Babylon. The first Beast in chap. xiii. is Mohammedanism, the death wound of which was inflicted by the Crusades. The false prophet is identified with the heretical sects. In the sixth part, Babylon is taken to be Rome sunk in secularism and vice, and the Beast is the devil. At the close of the sixth period the Church would be renewed by a return to apostolic poverty and simplicity through a new order of monks, or through two. These would be devoted to the contemplative life.

In most passages of the genuine writings, Joachim speaks only of one order of hermits clad in black. But in some he speaks also of two orders, one of which would represent martyrs to truth, and the other would devote itself to the refutation of heretics.

It is a remarkable coincidence that this last

prediction of Joachim's was speedily fulfilled in
the rise of the Franciscans and Dominicans;
and this fulfilment naturally won influence
and notoriety for Joachim's works. Joachim
came soon to be regarded as a prophet,
especially by the more fanatical section of the
Franciscans. These, owing to the secularisation
and corruption of the Papacy, became anti-
ecclesiastical and anti-papal, and gave Joachim's
prophecies an anti-papal character which their
author never intended. For of Joachim's
personal loyalty to the Church of Rome there
was no question. The Papacy was to him as
to Dante, only antichristian in its secularised
form. In its true and ideal sense it belonged,
according to Joachim, to the eternal order of
the Church. But the Franciscan zealots soon
came to make no distinction between the
ideal of the Papacy and its realisation in
history.

I have above observed that one of Joachim's
prophecies was speedily fulfilled in the rise of
the Franciscans and Dominicans, and that thus
his system received, as it were, a divine *im-
primatur*. But in another direction Joachim's
whole system was shaken to its foundation
by events which did not correspond to his
predictions. The Emperor Frederick II., to
whom so important a rôle was assigned in

this system, died in 1250, and thereby the triumph of the Papacy over the Empire became complete. But Joachim had predicted to this emperor a reign of 70 or 72 years, and a corresponding Babylonish captivity of 70 years to the Church. Ten years later another great disillusionment followed. In 1260 the second world era—that of the Son— was to come to an end and that of the Spirit begin. But this year came and went, and the Church and the world went their accustomed ways.

It is well worth observing that within 50 years after Joachim's death pseudepigraphical Commentaries on Jeremiah and Isaiah bearing Joachim's name became current, fiercely attacking the Papacy and glorifying the Franciscans and Dominicans as the saviours of the world, and in the *Liber Introductorius* of Gerard von Borgo San Donnino the writings of Joachim are declared to be the eternal Gospel mentioned in the Apocalypse. Peter John Olivi, another follower of Joachim, pronounced the Papacy to be the mystical Antichrist, and Ubertino di Casale identified the first Beast in chap. xiii. with Boniface VIII., and the second with Benedict XI., and confirms the identification of the latter by showing that according to the value of the Greek letters βενεδικτος (= 2 +

$5 + 50 + 5 + 4 + 10 + 20 + 300 + 70 + 200) =$
666, the number of the Antichrist.

I must again turn aside, to show how opportune for the progress of things spiritual and things temporal, was the work of Joachim of Floris and his successors. From its attack on the Papacy on the religious side, it gave encouragement alike to the kings and statesmen, who resisted the temporal encroachments of Rome, and to the men of thought and religious life, who resisted its intellectual and spiritual encroachments. (Up to the twelfth century the intellectual needs of men had found complete satisfaction within the Church. But from the thirteenth century onwards the more advanced thinkers began to break with the orthodox forms and views of Catholicism. The services which Catholicism had rendered to civilisation by the moral force it had inspired in the race, and by its organisation of the most heterogeneous elements into the forms from which every modern institution is constituted, are practically incommensurable. But the supremacy of Mediæval Catholicism could clearly only be transitory ; and her attitude of immobility could only be maintained by the entire suppression of every forward movement of the intellect.)

Accordingly with the revival of learning,

Catholicism, which, heretofore, had led the van in every department of human thought and energy, now made a retrograde movement, and sought to arrest the expansion of the human mind, and curb every effort after liberty and thought. This change in the attitude of the Church first shows itself in the twelfth century, and found concrete expression in the official establishment of the Inquisition by Innocent III. between 1198 and 1207, who as a jurist assimilated the crime of high treason against God to high treason against the civil ruler. In the next year followed the massacre of the Albigenses, and the principle of coercion was formally enunciated at the Fourth Lateran Council (1215), whereby rulers were required "to swear a public oath to exterminate all those who were branded as heretics by the Church." The Papacy reached its zenith under Innocent III. (1198–1216). In his inaugural sermon he declared: "I am the Vicar of Jesus Christ, the successor of Peter, and I am placed between God and man, less than God, but greater than man: I judge all men, but I can be judged of none."

Now there is a strange irony in the fact, that possibly at the very time Innocent was making these preposterous claims, antagonistic to all true progress in religion, in thought

and in science, Joachim may have been record-
ing his prediction that a pope would be Antichrist.   However this may be, he had at all
events finished wholly or in part his Commentary on St. John, from which every class
of men—statesmen, thinkers, monks, students,
artisans, and men of the world generally drew for
generations strength and courage to press onward
towards the better time, and to resist, in their
diverse ways, the claims of the Papacy, which
stood between them and the promised City of God.

In fact, in the thirteenth and fourteenth
centuries the Apocalypse was used as the chief
weapon of offence against the Church of Rome.
The Wycliffites in England, the Hussites in
Bohemia, the Waldenses, the Kathari and
others were all at one in applying the prophecies of the Antichrist in the Apocalypse to
the Papacy.   Each reckoned according to his
own fancy, and their interpretations were the
offspring of unbridled imagination.   But while
the extreme Franciscans and other religious
confraternities identified Rome with the Antichrist, the papal scholars retorted by condemning
their assailants as the collective Antichrist, both
sides using equally indefensible methods of
interpretation.

This unbounded licence in the interpretation
of the Apocalypse, which is the natural and

inevitable result of the dominant method of interpretation, *i.e.* the allegorical and mystical, was not confined to theologians and theological questions. Strangely enough, the Apocalypse won through this misuse public and even political significance in the Middle Ages, and became an actual force in moulding the history of the times. Thus, when Innocent III. summoned the Church in the West to undertake a new Crusade, he declared officially that the Saracens were, according to the Apocalypse, the true Antichrist, and Mohammed the false Prophet; and that the end of their power was at hand, since its duration was limited to 666 years, which should elapse from the appearance of Antichrist in Mohammed.

At a later date, Gregory IX., when at strife with the Hohenstaufen Emperor Frederick II., condemned him as the Beast mentioned in chap. xiii. risen from the sea full of names of blasphemy. The same Emperor, however, retorted in apocalyptic language : "The Pope himself is the great dragon who has seduced all the world, the Antichrist whose forerunner he has declared me to be" (Gieseler, *Eccl. Hist.* iii. 102, Eng. trans.). I have dwelt, perhaps, at disproportionate length on Joachim's and the related schools of interpretation because of their paramount influence in questions of Church

and Social Reform. The common people looked
to the coming seventh age predicted by Joachim
for deliverance from the tyrannies and cor-
ruptions of Church and State, and the strongest
weapons for assailing such evils were forged by
the students of the Apocalypse. The ferment
spread with every decade in depth and extent,
till at last from the spiritual and intellectual
travail of the ages the Reformation came to the
birth. When the reformed Churches had once
consolidated themselves, the interest in the
prophecies of the Apocalypse declined, though
its study was still vigorously pursued, partly
with polemical and partly with dogmatic aims.

Let us now summarise briefly the different
character and effects of the two chief schools of
interpretation. In the hands of Tyconius and
his followers the Spiritualising Method together
with the Recapitulation Theory was applied
with such thoroughness as to remove from the
Apocalypse nearly every reference to contemporary events—that is, events contemporary
with the individual expositor or the original
author, and so to destroy its significance for
its own immediate age or any other. The
interpretation thus became abstract and un-
related to the actual events of history, and the
Church, ceasing to feel itself hampered by its
prophecies, became self-satisfied, and its secu-

larisation went on apace. Thus the work of
this school, which could identify the 1000
years' reign of the saints with the 1000 years
of the Church's history, contributed without
doubt to its carnal security and its spiritual
stagnation.

A very different result followed on the
efforts of Joachim and other workers of similar
type. The eschatological school of Joachim,
which was based on a revival of the methods
of Irenæus and Victorinus with borrowings of
details from the school of Tyconius, found the
events of their own day mystically shadowed
forth as well as the impending end of the
world. The growing demoralisation of the
Church tended in itself to justify in some
measure the later writings of this school, which
boldly identified Rome with the Scarlet Woman
and the Pope with the Antichrist. Convinced
that these predictions were at last fulfilled in
Rome, hosts of students of the Apocalypse were
emboldened to spiritual rebellion against her.
The elements of such rebellion were present
everywhere, and so the ferment, social and
ecclesiastical, grew in volume till, as we have
already remarked, from the threatening chaos
the Reformation emerged, securing liberty of
conscience for religious men and liberty of
thought for men of science.

In the sixteenth century, when this movement had fully asserted itself, we shall find that
the Reformers followed in the main two different
methods of interpretation : The first is the
Church- or World-Historical, initiated by Petrus
Aureolus and adopted by Luther, the second
the Recapitulation Method of Joachim's school
with an intensified anti-papal bias but without
Chiliasm.

§ 5. *Church-Historical Method.*

The first method, the Church- or World-
Historical, originated in the fourteenth century.
This method was present in germ in the historically applied Recapitulation Theory.   It
was in effect an application to the whole
Apocalypse of the principle that Joachim and
others had applied to each division of it.   Its
two founders were Petrus Aureolus (1317) and
Nicolaus of Lyra (1329).   These found in the
Apocalypse a history of the Church's fortunes
prefigured in the actual order of its occurrence,
and not the same events continually rehandled
as in the Recapitulation Theory.   This method
was adopted by Luther, who combined with it
a strong anti-papal polemic.   This latter element,
it is worth observing, he drew from an English-
man named Purvey, a disciple of Wycliffe,
whose *Commentary on the Apocalypse*, Luther

published in the year 1528. In 1534, Luther
gave a short and brilliant but entirely fanciful
interpretation of the entire Apocalypse in his
preface to his translation. The first three
chapters he interprets with sound tact in their
natural sense, but from chap. iv. onwards
his method is just as arbitrary as that of his
predecessors. Luther's views long dominated
the interpretation of the Apocalypse within the
Lutheran Church, and are reproduced by such
writers as Bugenhagen, Funke, Osiander, and
Calovius, the two first of whom take the angel
with the eternal Gospel as prefiguring Luther.
In this school the Apocalypse was regarded as a
prophetic *Compendium of Church History*.

Of writers independent of Luther who nevertheless used the Church-Historical Method
and gave it an anti-papal character, might be
mentioned Lambertus, who shows Chiliastic
elements, Hoffmann, Marloratus, Bullinger and
Bibliander (1549). This last-named scholar is
thoroughly eclectic, but highly interesting.
He finds in the seven seals the history of this
world from Adam to its close, in the trumpets
a recapitulation, in the woman in chap. xii.
the Church which bears Christ, the first persecution of her children being by the Jews and
the second by Nero. The Beast he interprets
as the Roman Empire, its wound as Nero's

death, which is healed by the accession of
Vespasian.   Here we have elements of the
original   Contemporary - Historical   Method.
From this point onwards his interpretation
degenerates into the usual anti-papal distortion
of the text.

With the followers of the Church-Historical
Method we might mention the English scholar
Brightman.   This scholar interprets after this
method i.–x., but finds in xi.–xiv. a recapitulation of the same period as i.–x. from a different
point of view.

Also the French bishop and theologian
Bossuet (1690).   The work of the latter is
strongly propapal and anti-reformation.   He
finds in Gog and Magog the prediction of the
invasion of Europe by the Turks and the heresy
of Luther.

The followers of Bossuet, Aubert de Versé
and de Sacy, might here be mentioned, though
their works were not published till the beginning of the eighteenth century.   The former
has some interesting interpretations.   He as-
cribes the Apocalypse to Nero's time, and limits
its prophecies to the Roman Church.   Chap.
xi. he refers to the destruction of Jerusalem, in
xii. he finds the beginnings of Christianity, and
in xiii. sources of the great crises of the Roman
Empire.   The second Beast he takes to be the

heathen priesthood. The sixth head is Nero.
The outlook extends to Attila.   Aubert's
method is eclectic.   It embraces elements of
the Contemporary-Historical, World-Historical
and Eschatological Methods.

§ 9. *We now come to the second chief school of in-*
terpretation amongst the Reformers, the
Recapitulation Method in an embittered
anti-papal form but non-Chiliastic.

All reformers did not apply the World-
Historical Method to the interpretation of the
Apocalypse. Many learned scholars fell back
on the Recapitulation Theory which had been
used with such success by Joachim and his
school. The anti-papal tone which had marked
the successors of Joachim became in these
writers the dominant characteristic. They did
not, however, adopt the Chiliastic views of this
school. From this they were debarred by the
Augsburg and Helvetic Confessions, which
branded Chiliasm as a Judaistic heresy.
Amongst these scholars might be mentioned
Conradi (1560), Saskerides, Collado (1581) and
Paræus (1618) on the Continent, and Foxe
(1586) and Napier (1593) in Great Britain.
Of these Collado held that the seven seals, the
seven trumpets, and the seven bowls referred to
nearly the same events.   Into the characteristic

suppositions of this school we cannot naturally enter here. Arbitrariness reigns supreme. Under the World-Historical Method the exegete was bound by certain laws of sequence. Even from these last fetters of law and order is the Recapitulationist exempt. The hopelessness of arriving at any settled and reasonable results from these methods became manifest in certain quarters at an early date. Thus Calvin abstained from writing a Commentary on the Apocalypse, and Scaliger, one of the greatest Classics of the sixteenth century, who also declined the task, used frequently to say — *Calvinus sapit quod in Apocalypsin non scripsit.*

Through the application of this method the Apocalypse became the theatre for the exercise of a perverse ingenuity, on which one arbitrary interpretation had hardly established itself, when it was dislodged by another, no less arbitrary. Moreover, amongst Protestant continental scholars who were dominated by this theory, the possibilities of a right interpretation of chap. xx. was denied them, since in the Augsburg and Helvetic Confessions, Chiliastic views were condemned as heretical. Since no such veto existed in England, we shall find that amidst all the grotesque, unscientific and fanatical anti-papal exegesis of our countrymen,

this fragment of the right interpretation was in
the main preserved.

§ 7. *Rise of the Philological School.*

Contemporaneously with the schools of interpretation just dealt with, there was a third
destined to become in time a very important
school, which devoted itself all but exclusively
to the philological study of the Apocalypse.
To this school belonged Camerarius (1556),
Beza (1556), Castellio (1583), Drusius (1612)
and others in the seventeenth century. A
feeling of despair as to ever arriving at the
real meaning of the Apocalypse had no little
share in giving birth to this school. Camerarius
writes : " Since an actual faculty of vaticination
is requisite in order to discover the meaning of
predictions still unfulfilled, the Greek verse
interpreted by Cicero as *Bene qui conjiciet,*
vatem hunc perhibete optimum ('call the good
guesser the best seer'), is especially applicable
here."

§ 8. *Revival of Contemporary and*
Eschatological Methods.

But while success appeared hopeless, and no
interpretation could justify itself as more than
a mere conjecture to the critical judgment, the
way towards a scientific exegesis was being

prepared by a break with the World-Historical and Spiritualising Methods and a return to those of Irenæus, Hippolytus and Victorinus on the part of some Jesuit scholars—Hentenius, Ribeira, Salmeron, Pereyra, Alcasar, Juan Mariana, and others.

The polemical interpretations of the Reformers directed against Rome naturally drew forth rejoinders from its leading scholars, and by far the most effective and scientific emanated from the Jesuits just mentioned. These writers returned to a literal interpretation of the text, and attempted in some degree to understand the contents of the book from the standpoint of the author : they sought to prove that the time of the Antichrist was still in the distant future, and interpreted the prophecy of the Babylonian whore of heathen Rome with a view to the greater glorification of Rome Christian.

It is possible that this return to the methods of Irenæus and Victorinus may have been suggested by the use that Bibliander and Bullinger made of these early Fathers. However this may be, a breach was made with the World-Historical and Spiritualising and Recapitulation Methods, and at the same time the beginning or rather the revival of a partially scientific exposition of the Apocalypse.

3

A forerunner of this school was Hentenius
(1547), who in a preface to an edition of
Arethas tried to show that chaps. vi.–xi. dealt
with the overthrow of the Synagogue, and
xii.–xix. with the destruction of heathenism
under the figure Babylon. Salmeron (1614)
took the same view, and agreed with Hentenius
that the Apocalypse was written before the
fall of Jerusalem. He refused, however, to
write a Commentary on the Apocalypse, and
compared such an undertaking with an attempt
to square the circle. But two names of great
merit stand forth from the rest in this school,
namely Ribeira (*ob.* 1591) and Alcasar (1614).
The former argues rightly that the author
prophesies only of his own time and the last
times. The first five seals began with the
preaching of Christ, and end with Trajan's
persecution. In the sixth seal (vi. 12) the
author passes on to the signs of the last time,
which are still to come, even for Ribeira.
Babylon he identified with Rome—not merely
Rome pagan, but also Rome in the last days,
when it would break with the Roman See (see
Ribeira (ed. 1593), p. 282 sqq.). Alcasar, like
his predecessor Hentenius, regards chaps. vi.–xi.
as dealing with the conflict of the Church
with Judaism, xii. – xix. as forecasting the
conflict with heathenism, and xx.–xxii. as

describing Rome's triumph and dominion. The woman in chap. xii. is the Jewish Christian community which bears the Gentile Church. This Church is forthwith persecuted by the Roman Empire. The first Beast is the Roman Empire, the second is $\dot{\eta}$ $\dot{a}\lambda a\zeta o\nu \epsilon i a$ $\beta i o\nu$ (= " the pride of life ") = 666. The head, that had seemed dead and had revived, was Domitian, who recalled the Nero of the past. Constantine was the angel who bound Satan. Thereupon the Millennium began. xix. 11 sqq. represent the complete conversion of the Roman Empire and the present glory and authority of papal Rome. Alcasar dedicates his work to Pope Paul, and exults that he has been the first to bring this light out of the darkness of the Apocalypse. Unfortunately for Alcasar, whatever fragments of the true interpretation he may have recovered from the earlier chapters, it is just from chap. xii. where he adopts the World-Historical Method that his exegesis becomes subjective, and the contribution, that he esteemed of most importance, is really of no value whatever.

Before we leave this section we might mention Mariana (1619), who interprets the death wound of the Beast of Nero's suicide, as originally did Victorinus; and the healing of this wound, of the belief in Nero's return from the East. The seven trumpets refer to different heretics, and the fifth to Luther.

As the recovery of the Chiliastic interpretation of the Apocalypse by Joachim and his followers was the chief scientific contribution of the thirteenth century to the exegesis of the Apocalypse, so the recovery and application of the Contemporary-Historical Theory by the Jesuits was the chief scientific contribution of the end of the sixteenth and the beginning of the seventeenth century.

§ 9. *From these schools we pass on to extravagant developments of the Recapitulation and Chiliastic Methods: and to the rise of the Literary-Critical in the seventeenth century.*

From Ribeira's and Alcasar's Commentaries their religious opponents in Germany could have learnt a more excellent way of exegesis. Nay more, from their fellow-religionist Bibliander, who was earlier than either, they might have gleaned the elements of a better method, but the dread of the Papacy blinded as yet the eyes of nearly all Protestant scholars. No method that obliged them to abandon an anti-papal interpretation of the Apocalypse could gain a hearing save from a solitary scholar or two. It is true that the scholars of the sixteenth

century were justified in maintaining that the
Apocalypse dealt with Rome, but in insisting
that it was Rome papal they were wrong, but
after all not so extravagantly wrong as Alcasar,
who made the extraordinary discovery that the
secret aim of the Apocalypse was to denounce
heathen and glorify papal Rome.

Matters being so, the choice of methods,
especially for continental Protestants, was very
limited. They could not revert to a Chiliastic
interpretation ; for such views were heretical
according to the Articles of their Churches :
nor could they accept the Contemporary-
Historical Method ; for this would necessitate
their abandonment of an anti-papal interpretation : nor, finally, could they use the
World - Historical interpretation, since this
method had become discredited through its unbounded arbitrariness and utter barrenness of
assured results. Thus their choice was limited
to the Recapitulation Theory, unless they broke
with their Church symbols, or discovered a new
method of interpretation. We shall find, as we
proceed, that Protestant scholars on the Continent as a matter of fact did both. They revived
the Chiliastic doctrine with a vigour never displayed in earlier times, and they initiated the
beginnings of the Literary Critical Method.

But before we deal with these we must

mention Crocius, Hofmann, and Coccejus, notable scholars of this century, who still clung to the Recapitulation Theory. In the hands of Coccejus (1668), the Recapitulation Theory was carried to the most extravagant lengths. History runs parallel courses not only in the seven seals, the seven trumpets and the seven bowls, but even in the account of the seven Churches. The Millennium belonged to the past. A similar, though more reasonable form of the Recapitulation Theory, was advanced by Marckius towards the close of this century.

But turning from this thoroughly antiquated method, we are met with the most vigorous, though not the most judicious, school of interpretation of this century, that is, the Chiliastic. This method, which could flourish openly in England, but which was branded as Judaistic on the Continent, as we have already pointed out, by the Confessions of the Lutheran and Reformed Churches, had always been popular among the continental heretics, especially after its revival by Joachim. Its chief English representative was Mede (1627 and 1632), whose views on the synchronism existing between the first nine chapters and the rest of the book — the former dealing with the destinies of the Empire, the latter with those of the Church—were adopted widely in England and were reproduced also in Germany. The theory is difficult to characterise, but it may from one standpoint be regarded as a species of the Recapitulation Method. Mede's chief English disciples were Sir Isaac Newton and Whiston. The latter, like many of his predecessors, ventured to predict the year on which the Millennium would begin. First he fixed on 1715 and next on 1734 as the year in question; but as he had the misfortune to survive both these dates, a fresh study of his data and no doubt a larger prudence made him relegate this date to 1866—beyond the reach of his own or the next two generations. Amongst Mede's German disciples were Peganius—a *nom de guerre*—and Vitringa (1705). The latter adopted in part the Recapitulation System of Coccejus, with the Chiliastic interpretation of Mede, and found the entire history of the Church foretold in the first six seals, but in the interpretation of the trumpets, the bowls, the Beast and the 1000 years he appears to be dependent on Mede. Through this influential work, Chiliasm became popular in the *pietistic* circles of Germany, despite the ban of the Augsburg Confession.

Other adherents of this school were Abbadie, Lange (1730) and Bengel (1740, etc.).

Lange interprets the whole Apocalypse from chap. iv. onwards eschatologically. Bengel is wildly Chiliastic—in fact he finds a double Millennium predicted—the first from 1836 to 2836 when Satan would be bound, and the second from 2836 to 3836, *i.e.* the true Millennium and the final judgment. With Bengel's work, Chiliasm finally emerged from the ban of the Lutheran Church.

From this triumphant and extravagant assertion of Chiliasm we must turn now to the most interesting movement in the seventeenth century which took its rise from Grotius (1644); *i.e.*

§ 10. *The discovery of the Literary-Critical Method and the adoption of the Contemporary-Historical Method by Protestant Scholars.*

The most notable contribution, next to those of the Jesuit scholars of the seventeenth century, was made by the Dutch scholar Grotius. Grotius' interpretation of the Apocalypse was of a very eclectic character. It diverges from that of earlier scholars of the Reformation in that it ignores wholly the current anti-papal interpretation. This is the first ground for distinction. This advance he may have owed in part to Bibliander, whose work contains so

many fresh contributions to a better knowledge
of the Apocalypse; but it was certainly due in
the main to his use of the Jesuit Alcasar. For,
like Alcasar, he divides the book into three
parts: chaps. vi.–xi. the Judgment on Judaism,
xii.–xix. the judgment on heathenism, xx.–xxii.
the condition of the Church since Constantine.
With chap. xiv. Grotius, like Alcasar, passes
from the Contemporary - Historical to the
World-Historical Method. His independent
attempts at a detailed interpretation of the
Apocalypse cannot be called happy. According
to Grotius, chap. xi. refers to the troubles occa-
sioned by Barcochba in the reign of Trajan.
The first two-thirds of chap. xii. are a description of Simon Magus, who is an instrument of
the Dragon, or Satan. The seven heads of
the Beast are the seven Emperors, beginning
with Claudius and ending with Titus. In xii.
13 begins the persecution of Nero; in xii.
17 that of Domitian. The number 666 means
Ulpius—part of the name of Trajan. Yet
when he comes to xvii. 11 this Beast is said
to be Domitian, since he was known as the
bald Nero—Calvus Nero. It is not by his
detailed interpretation, of which I have given
a few specimens, that Grotius established a
claim to remembrance in connection with the
Apocalypse, but by two new departures which

he made. He was the first Protestant scholar
to break definitely with the anti-papal interpretation, and to lead the way towards the
recovery of the Contemporary - Historical
Method. In this respect, of course, he was
not original; for he was only adopting the
sounder method revived by Bibliander and
the Jesuits. But in the second departure he
was original. Observing that certain portions
of the Apocalypse presupposed different
historical relations, and that tradition itself
was divided as to the place and date of its
composition, he conjectured that the Apocalypse was composed of several visions written
down at different times and in different places,
some before and some after the destruction of
Jerusalem.

The earlier prophecies against Jerusalem
were written while the Seer was an exile in
Patmos under Claudius; the later prophecies
were written under Vespasian in Ephesus.
Thus Grotius thought the conflicting elements
in tradition and the text were satisfactorily
explained. In this theory of Grotius we have
the beginnings of a new method—that of the
Literary-Critical, which is so prominent in our
own day and without which several outstanding
difficulties of the Apocalypse cannot be solved.

Grotius was followed in England by Hammond ; but the time had not yet come when Grotius' real merits could be recognised.

Bengel and his school triumphantly held the field. Their wildest interpretations were eagerly welcomed by the religious public. Nothing was too fatuous for the prevailing taste.

Every expounder assumed the airs of a prophet, and the numbers and dates of the Apocalypse were the subject of the most fantastic theories. These groundless fancies found special acceptance in England, where Mede, Newton and Whiston had deepened the interest in Apocalyptic studies. Bengel's work was translated into English at the especial request of John Wesley, and thus became a dominant authority in this country amongst the most religious men of the time.

§ 11. *But unreason cannot maintain itself indefinitely : at last the Contemporary-Historical Method asserted itself in a thoroughgoing but in a limited and perverse form.*

Such was the prevailing attitude towards the Apocalypse till the middle of the eighteenth century. But the time was ripe for better things. The World - Historical and Church - Historical Methods had run their course, and so far from reaching any impregnable or generally accepted results, had established their incompetence on this field by their hopeless arbitrariness and unprofitableness. The Apocalyptic chronologisings, moreover, which had been rife in England and had subsequently been popularised on a gigantic scale by Bengel in Germany, had served to alienate the more intelligent from this and other popular methods of interpretation. But the most important event connected with such subjects was the rise of historical criticism in this century. It is remarkable that a century that gave birth to the most boundless subjectivism should have also called the historic sense into active existence. Hope at last dawns on the long journey we have taken down the centuries. From this time forward we can reckon, on the whole, on a steady advance towards the solution of the problem. Progress may have occasionally to be made by roundabout ways, wrong paths may for a time be pursued, side issues be mistaken for the problems-in-chief, and criticism thereby be obliged to retrace its steps after apparently spending its energies in vain. But, notwithstanding, possession in part of the promised land has been won, and its entire conquest is only a question of time.

Under the influence of this rising critical spirit in rude collision with the dominant methods of interpretation the bold thesis was advanced, that the prophecies of the Apocalypse, so far from embracing the entire history of the world or even of the Jewish or Christian Churches, were directed firstly and lastly against Jerusalem.

Thus the Apocalypse was interpreted in this school by the Contemporary-Historical Method in a very limited sense. The chief advocates of this view were Abauzit, Harduin, Wetstein, Harenberg, Herder and Züllig, writing from 1732 to 1840.

Great differences of interpretation exist among these critics, since the application of the Contemporary-Historical Method in such a limited sense forced its adherents to do violence repeatedly to the obvious sense of the text. Thus they discovered the seven hills to be in the neighbourhood of Jerusalem, the seven Churches within Jerusalem, the seven heads of the Beast in the Herodian kings, and other like perversities. Notwithstanding, the rightness of this method for the interpretation of the Apocalypse was recognised and the way prepared, and none too soon, for the fitter and adequate application of this method by Corrodi, Herrenschneider, Eichhorn, Bleek,

Ewald and others. None too soon, I repeat;
for in Reimarus, towards the end of the
eighteenth century, it is stated that "reasonable theologians prefer to refrain from the
seven sealed book and confess that of all its
wonderful visions they cannot with certainty
interpret a single one." A similar confession
is made by Schleiermacher.

§ 12. *But it was soon discovered that this
circumscribed application of this
method was untenable, and so scholars
passed on to the full and legitimate
application of the Contemporary-Historical Method without or with Chiliastic interpretation.*

According to this school of interpreters the
Apocalypse was directed against Judaism, and
against the Roman Empire and especially its
capital.

Corrodi, in his *Geschichte des Chiliasmus*
(1780), did much to help forward this method
of interpretation by explaining the Apocalypse
from Jewish Rabbinical writings, interpreting
the ten kings of the Parthians, and defending
the reference of the Antichrist to Nero. Herrenschneider (1786), in an Inaugural Dissertation
at Strassburg, expounded briefly this method
which Eichhorn applied in a learned commentary.

The most distinguished representatives of this school, such as Semler, Corrodi, Bleek, Ewald, De Wette, Lücke, Volkmar, conclude that xi. 1, 2 speaks of the preservation of the Temple. Hence the Apocalypse, if we assume its unity, was written before 70 A.D.

Since these two verses are of great importance in dating at all events a part of the book, I will here quote them. Rev. xi. 1, 2, "And there was given me a reed like unto a rod : and one said, Rise, and measure the temple of God and the altar, and them that worship therein. And the court which is without the temple leave without, and measure it not ; for it hath been given unto the nations : and the holy city shall they tread under foot forty and two months." The scholars above mentioned established as an assured result the fact that the Apocalypse was directed essentially against Rome, and, as a result practically beyond the reach of cavil, the identification of the Antichrist with Nero *redivivus*. This identification is notably confirmed by the interpretation of the mystical number 666, arrived at independently by four scholars in the nineteenth century, Fritzsche, Benary, Hitzig, and Reuss. These discovered that the value of the letters in Cæsar Nero, when written in Hebrew (קְסַר נְרוֹן), amounts to 666 ; and this discovery is corroborated by the

fact that in the Uncial MS. C, the two
Cursives 5 and 11, in Tyconius and the original
Armenian Version, the mystic number was
given not as 666, but as 616. The difference between 666 and 616 can at once be
explained on the above theory; for whereas
the Greeks spelt Nero with a final ν ($N\acute{\epsilon}\rho\omega\nu$), the
Latins, of course, did not. In the West and
the countries influenced by it, the omission
of this ν (which as a numeral = 50), reduced the
number 666 to 616. Finally, they universally
and rightly interpreted chap. xx. chiliastically,
and chap. xvi. generally of the Parthians. The
best account of this school is given by De Wette
(p. 7), " In so far as (the writer of the Apocalypse) reproves and admonishes in the prophetic
character, he manifestly takes this standpoint
in the Letters to the Seven Communities in
Asia Minor, the conditions of which he knows
so accurately and depicts so faithfully. But,
if we had some further knowledge of their
history, a clear representation of them would
lie before us. In so far as the writer of the
Apocalypse has the whole Church and its
future before his eyes, it is clear from a
multitude of passages that his chief impulse
to prophetic activity arose from his still vivid
impression of the Neronic persecution bound
up with the popular belief that this persecutor

of the Christians was still alive and would soon return as the fully realised Antichrist. As the chief enemy of the Christian Church, he recognised the idolatrous religious system of Rome supported by its world power and maintained by the devices of its priests. . . . It is not with the destruction of Jerusalem, which he does not look for, that he connects the hope of the victory of Christ . . . but of Rome; for Rome is for him the home—of the Antichrist, the new Babylon which must be destroyed, if the Christian faith is to triumph."

Here at last we have reached the right method with which to begin our study of the Apocalypse—to begin, I repeat; for other methods than the Contemporary-Historical and Eschatological are needed for its complete interpretation.

Before, however, we deal with these, we must turn aside for a brief notice of some modern representatives of antiquated methods in the beginning of the next lecture.

CHAPTER II.

HISTORY OF THE INTERPRETATION OF THE APOCALYPSE—*Concluded*.

BEFORE I enter on the fuller treatment of the methods which made real contributions to the interpretation of the Apocalypse, I must deal shortly with certain antiquated methods which have still their followers in the learned world, though they are often combined by them with one or more of the sounder methods of the past.

§ 13. *Of these we should perhaps mention first the "Astronomical [1] Method."*

This method was originally put forward by Dupuis in his *Origine de tous les Cultes*, first published in 1795. The edition which I have used is that of 1835, in ten volumes. The author devotes pp. 101–384 to an examination of the Apocalypse. While he doubts its authenticity, he does not apparently question its origin in the first century A.D.

---

[1] I have discovered since the above was written that in an anonymous work, entitled *Horus oder Astrognostisches Endurtheil über die Offenbarung Johannis*, 1783, this method was already adopted.

As regards its relation to astronomy or astrology, Dupuis connects the idea of the Seven Churches and the Seven Spheres, viii. 156 sq. He explains the woman in chap. xii. who is pursued by a serpent as a reflection of the constellation of the Virgin and the Serpent. Similarly, he seeks to explain why the numbers seven and twelve and the Lamb play so great a rôle in the Apocalypse, viii. 133.

This method has been recently revived in Germany by Jäger and Hommel. In *Reformation*, viii. 212–213, 1909, Hommel speaks of the brilliant discovery of Pastor Samuel Jäger, who claims to have detected allusions to the six intermediate constellations of the Zodiac, beginning with the Goat, in Apoc. viii. 13, ix. 3–10, 14, x., xi. 1, xii. 11 sqq., 3 sq. Hommel supplements Jäger's discovery by finding references to the last three, *i.e.* the Crab, Twins and Ox, in xiii. 1–10, 14, xv. 1, and to the first three, *i.e.* the Ram, Fish and Aquarius, in viii. 7, 8, 10.

This method was next advocated in the *Expositor*, 1911 (160–180, 210–230, 461–474, 504–519), in four articles, entitled *The Symbolical Language of the Apocalypse*, which are in part translated from the German of Dr. Johannes Lepsius, and in part written by Sir William Ramsay.

Dr. Lepsius holds that the Apocalypse is, in a certain sense, an astrological book; for it makes free use of the symbolical language of ancient Oriental astrology.

The Cherubim are "the four constellations which mark, according to the four quarters of the universe, the spring equinox, the summer solstice, the autumn equinox and the winter solstice" (p. 223)—*i.e.* the Lion, Ox, Water carrier, Scorpion. Again—" In the description of the twelve foundation stones of the celestial Jerusalem we meet with the colours of the standards of the twelve tribes (corresponding to the precious stones of the breastplate); for the twelve-gated celestial city, with its twelve-towered gates, is nothing else but the firmament, with the twelve gates of the firmament." Like many other scholars, he identifies the twenty-four elders with the twenty-four constellations of the northern and southern hemispheres, which, according to Diod. ii. 31, were called by the Babylonians "the judges over all things." Again, "as the twelve signs of the Zodiac are the guardian angels of the twelve tribes of Israel, so the seven planet angels are the guardian angels of the peoples and of the heathen-Christian communities" (p. 225); likewise, since, according to Josephus (*Bell. Jud.* v. 5. 5), the twelve shewbreads signify the twelve signs of the Zodiac, the Table of the Shewbread and the Candlesticks represent the community of God—of Israel and of the Gentiles. There are a great number of similar explanations, but we cannot deal with them here.

Ramsay writes with regard to Dr. Lepsius' theory that "the astronomical method, while it is a useful servant, must not be taken as a master and director" (p. 506); but in these articles his practice has not perhaps been as wise as his counsel; for he seems to have unduly committed himself to it.

Another work that has adopted this method was by a Russian, Nicolaus Morosow, published in 1907, and translated into German in 1912 under the title, *Die Offenbarung Johannis eine astronomish-historische Untersuchung*. The Introduction is furnished by Dr. Drews of Karlsruhe, whose credulity in regard to the fanciful and absurd varies in direct ratio to his scepticism in things historical.

Morosow claims to have established not only the year of the vision of the writer of the Apocalypse, *but even the actual day and hour in the year 395 A.D.* ! The writer was John Chrysostom. It speaks ill for Russia that 6000 copies of a book of this type should have been sold in one year, and still worse for the Russian Church that it felt itself obliged in

self-defence to have this book placed on the
Index by the State.

Morosow deduces the above date from two
alleged grounds. (1) The life of Chrysostom is
not intelligible save on the presupposition that
he wrote the Apocalypse. (2) The representation of the heaven given in the Apocalypse
corresponds exactly to what it appeared from
the island of Patmos in the evening of September
30, 395 A.D., and the like appearance has never
been witnessed from this island since the
Christian era. To (1) no scholar who knows
the Greek of the Apocalypse and that of
Chrysostom could agree.

As regards (2) the student who is acquainted
with Jewish and Christian apocalyptic will
regard the entire hypothesis as a grotesque
jeu d'esprit. That behind several of the figures
and conceptions in the Apocalypse lay astronomical ideas he will be the first to acknowledge, but he will at the same time be convinced
that to the Seer the astronomical origin of these
conceptions was in most cases wholly unknown.

§ 14. *Other antiquated methods, which are still
in some measure current, are the World-
Historical, the Church-Historical, and
the Symbolical-Historical.*

A combination of the first two methods is

to be found in the works of Hengstenberg
(1849–51), Ebrard and Elliott with a strong
anti-papal bias. The Apocalypse becomes a
prophetic compendium of the history of the
world and the Church. In the massive Commentary of Elliott we find a naïve confession
as to his chief auxiliary in the interpretation of
the Apocalypse, which is none other than
Gibbon's *History of the Decline and Fall of
the Roman Empire.*

But this system of exegesis was abandoned
by Auberlen (1874), to whom we owe the
Symbolical-Historical, according to which the
Apocalypse prophesies, not of individual
historical events, but of great turning points
in the struggle between light and darkness,
truth and falsehood, in the history of the
Church. Auberlen has been followed in this
country by Milligan and Archbishop Benson.

Others, like Von Hoffmann and Van Lorentz,
combined the Church-Historical and Symbolical-
Historical. Here we might place our learned
countryman Alford, who, together with these
methods, had recourse to a weakened form of
the Recapitulation Theory. His interpretation
is chiliastic, like other members of this school,
and also anti-papal.

Next we have the Eschatological Method,
adopted in its integrity by Kliefoth (1874),

Lange, Zahn, and Roman Catholic scholars as Stern, Kremenz and Waller.

Lastly, we must mention in a class by itself the recent valuable and learned Commentary by Dr. Swete. This writer, who maintains the literary unity of the Apocalypse to the complete exclusion of the use of sources, follows at one time the Contemporary-Historical, at another the World-Historical and Church-Historical Methods, at another the Symbolical-Historical, and at another the Eschatological (p. ccxviii). While some of these methods are indispensable, others have made no contribution to the interpretation of the Apocalypse. They may be used, indeed, for purposes of edification, and can rightly be so used, but we must remember that in seeking to interpret the Apocalypse we are seeking to discover what the Apocalypse meant to its writer and its earliest readers, who were in touch with him.

§ 15. *Of the methods hitherto dealt with, the only methods that have made a permanent contribution are the Contemporary-Historical and Eschatological, and in a minor degree the Philological.*

From the Contemporary-Historical Method we have learnt that the Apocalypse is directed

mainly against the heathen Empire of Rome
supported by its heathen priesthood, that
Nero *redivivus* is the wounded head, that it
is Nero Cæsar that is referred to in the
mystical number 666, and, finally, that the
Temple was still standing when xi. 1, 2 was
written.

It thus follows that the date of the
Apocalypse, according to this school, was about
67–68 or thereabouts. And if the absolute
unity of the Apocalypse be assumed, there is
no possibility, I think, of evading this conclusion.[1]

But if we accept 68 as the date of the
entire work, there are many passages which
are hopelessly inexplicable ; for these just as
inevitably postulate a date subsequent to 70
A.D. as xi. 1, 2 in its original setting postulates
a date anterior to it. If, then, the possibilities
of exegesis were exhausted in the methods
already dealt with, science would have to
relegate portions of the Apocalypse to the limbo

[1] W. M. Ramsay in his admirable commentary on *The Letters
to the Seven Churches* (1904), holds apparently to the absolute
unity of the Apocalypse, and yet at the same time accepts the
Domitianic date. But the Contemporary-Historical Method
combined with the Eschatological is not adequate to the task
of explaining the Apocalypse. Hort (in his posthumous work,
The Apocalypse of St. John, i.–iii., published in 1908 but really
written as early as 1879) accepts the absolute unity of the
Apocalypse and yet maintains the early date.

of unsolved and unsolvable problems. But
there is no such *impasse*. In the New
Testament Apocalypse there is not that rigid
unity of authorship and consistency of detail
that the past has presupposed. Within recent
years it has been proved to demonstration by
the methods of *Literary Criticism* that most
of the Old Testament legalistic and prophetic
books are composite, and the same fact has
been established with regard to the Apocalyptic
Literature, to which literature the New Testament Apocalypse itself belongs. Some of the
Jewish Apocalypses, like the Ascension of
Isaiah, betray the handiwork of successive
editors, and are accordingly to be explained
on the *Redactional Hypothesis*. Others, like
the Ethiopic Book of Enoch (or 1 Enoch),
exhibit a series of independent sources connected more or less loosely together, and are
to be explained on the *Sources Hypothesis*.
Others again, like the Testaments of the XII
Patriarchs and the Book of Jubilees, manifest
an undoubted unity of authorship, though the
author has from time to time drawn from other
sources, and has not always assimilated these
fragmentary elements to their new contexts.
Such works are to be explained on the *Fragmentary Hypothesis*. Now scholars have in
recent years applied with varying success these

three hypothesis with a view to the solution of
the N. T. Apocalypse.

We have now come to the parting of the
ways. All the preceding methods presupposed
an absolutely rigid unity of authorship. This
supposition we must now abandon, if we are
to gain further insight into the problems of
the N. T. Apocalypse.

§ 16. *Literary-Critical Method proceeding on
the Redactional Hypothesis, the Sources
Hypothesis, and the Fragmentary
Hypothesis.*

1. *The Redactional Hypothesis.*—The literary criticism of Grotius was resumed by Vogel
(1811–16), and later by Bleek, but it was not
till Weizsäcker reopened the question in 1882
that the problem was seriously undertaken by
his pupil Völter. The views of this writer
have passed through at least three stages (*Die
Entstehung d. Apok.*,[2] 1885 ; *Die Offenbarung
Johannis—Keine ursprünglich jüdische Apok.*,
1886, *Das Problem d. Apok.*, 1893 ; *Die
Offenbarung Johannis*, 1904), in the course of
which he has abandoned a purely Redactional
Hypothesis for a Sources Hypothesis plus a
redaction.

According to Völter's final views there are in
the Apocalypse two sources, which were edited

by a Christian in the reign of Trajan, and
subsequently revised in Hadrian's time by
another writer. To the last we owe i. 9–iii.
22, in other words, the letters to the Seven
Churches and a few other verses; to the editor
in Trajan's time passages in twelve of the
chapters, amounting in some cases only to
single verses or phrases, in others to sections
of four verses, six, eight or more. Of the two
sources, one — the original Apocalypse — was
written by John, whose surname was Mark, in
the year 60 A.D., and the other by the heretic
Cerinthus in 70 A.D. It is unnecessary here
to enter further into the details of Völter's
hypothesis, as it has failed to gain the suffrages
of critical scholars,—in fact, as a whole it has
been rejected on every hand. On the other
hand, Völter has shown much insight in his
individual criticisms. For instance, he was the
first to point out the radical difference in outlook and authorship between vii. 1–8 and vii.
9–17, the original meaning of xiv. 14–20, and
the true character of x.–xi. 13 as an interlude
introduced between ix. 21 and xi. 14 ; for
originally xi. 14 followed immediately on ix. 21.
In 1891, Erbes (*Die Offenbarung Johannis*)
maintained that the book was entirely of
Christian origin — the groundwork written
originally in 62. With this a Caligula-Apoca-

lypse was subsequently incorporated and the
entire work revised about 80.

The same method was applied from quite
a different standpoint by Vischer (*Die Offenbarung Johannis, eine jüdische Apocalypse in
Christlichen Bearbeitung*, 1886; 2nd edition,
1895), whose work was introduced to the
notice of the learned world by Harnack. As
opposed to Völter and Erbes, who maintained
the essentially Christian character of the
sources, Vischer was of opinion that the book
was essentially Judaistic and not Christian
originally, and that it was subsequently edited by
a Christian who added the letters to the Seven
Churches, and certain words, phrases, verses or
passages in chaps. v. 6, 8, 9–14, vi. 1, 16, vii.
9–17, ix. 11, xi. 8*b*, 15, xii. 11, xiii. 9–10, xiv.
1–5, 10, 12, 13, xv. 3, xvi. 15, xvii. 6, 14, xix.
7, 9, 10, 13*b*, xx. 4, 5, 6, xxi. 5*b*–8, 14*b*,
xxii. 6–21. Vischer was of opinion that
chaps. xi.–xii., which constitute the heart of
the Apocalypse, were decisive for this view.
According to chap. xi., the Sanctuary of the
Jewish Temple was to remain intact, and
according to chap. xii., the Messiah was not
to be born till the end was at hand, and was to
be carried forthwith to heaven and preserved
in safety there. This is, Vischer insists, the
Synagogue and not the Christian Church that

is speaking. When once the letters to the
Seven Churches and the rest of the Christian
additions are removed, there remain, according
to Vischer, a purely Jewish writing, which
formed a unity in itself, and was translated
from a Hebrew original. The similarity in
the style in the Christian additions to that of
the original Jewish section, Vischer explains
by the hypothesis that the author of the additions was also the translator of the original.

This clever hypothesis found a wide acceptance at the time; but, as Bousset urges, it
cannot be regarded as satisfactory; for Vischer,
in the first place, has not succeeded in proving
the Jewish character of xi.–xii., nor justified his
fundamental thesis as to the unity of the book.

Before passing on, however, we should
observe that the same year that Vischer's
first edition appeared, Weyland's brochure
(*Theol. Studien*, 1886, 454 sqq.; and *Omwerkings-en Compilatie-Hypothesen toegepast
op de Apokalypse van Johannes*, 1888) was
published, in which a somewhat similar hypothesis was set forth. He, like Vischer, finds in
the Apocalypse two Jewish sources. The first
was written under Titus, and embraces some
verses in chap. i., chaps. iv.–ix., xi. 14–18,
some verses in xiv., xv., xvi., chaps. xvii.–
xviii., parts of xix. – xxi. and chap. xxii.

The second was written under Nero, and embraces x.–xi. 13, xii., xx. and certain verses in xv., xvi., xix., xx., xxi.

A Christian editor added the Seven Letters, the beginning and end of the book, and a succession of interpolations. The passages attributed to the Christian editor coincide for the most part with those assigned to him by Vischer. Weyland rightly, like Völter, recognises the nature of x.–xi. 13, but has not made any permanent contribution. A few Christian scholars have given their adhesion to Vischer's hypothesis, or adopted similar hypotheses, such as those of Iselin, Rovers and O. Holtzmann; but I venture to predict that Vischer's and kindred hypotheses will ultimately fail to find acceptance among critics of the first order. From an inadequate knowledge of the text such views are still set before the public. Of these I shall briefly discuss the theories of Kohler, Weiss and Von Soden. Kohler, a learned Jewish scholar, in 1905 wrote an article on the Apocalypse in the *Jewish Encyclopædia* (x. 390–396), in which he follows, in the main, in the footsteps of Vischer, and that so closely, that there is only a difference of treatment in detail. Kohler does not assume one Jewish original, but at least two. The first consists of parts of i. 1,

8, 12–19, iv.–ix., and xi. 14–18, and was written in Hebrew before the fall of Jerusalem.

The second, of x. 2–xi. 13, xii.–xiii., xiv. 6–xxii. 6, which was written in Hebrew during the siege and after the fall of Jerusalem. These two apocalypses were in the possession of the Essenes, who joined the Christian Church, and were adapted for Christian use by an early Christian. "Possibly," he writes, "the Seer of Patmos, when writing the letters to the seven churches, or one of his disciples when sending them out, had these apocalypses before him, and incorporated them into his work. This fact," he thinks, "would account for the striking similarities in expression between the first three chapters and the remainder."

I have given Kohler's hypothesis longer consideration than it deserves, because it comes from a Jewish source. Kohler's hypothesis throws no fresh light on the problem, while it fails to apprehend the general unity of thought and style that characterise the book. Like Völter, there is a use here of the Redaction combined with the Sources Hypothesis.

The next critic who calls for notice, *i.e.* Johannes Weiss, is one of the most brilliant of the New Testament scholars of the present day. His works, *Die Offenbarung des Johannis; Die Schriften des neuen Testa-*

ments, ii. 597–684, published in 1904 and 1908 respectively, cannot any more than Völter's last work or Weyland's treatise be strictly classed under the heading of the Redaction Hypothesis ; for, like Völter's and Weyland's, they assume sources.

The first source was the original Johannine Apocalypse, written in the second half of the year 60 A.D., consisting of parts of chap. i., chaps. ii.–vii., some verses in viii. 1–5, 13, chap. ix., xii. 7–12, xiii. 11–18, xiv. 1–5, 14–20, xx.–xxi. 4, xxii. 3–5, 8*a*, 11–13, 14*a*, 15, 16, 20. The second source was Jewish and composite, and issued in the year 70, and consists of x., xi. 1–13, xii. 1–6, 14–17, xiii. 1–7, xv.–xix., xxi. 5–27, xxii. 6, 7, 8*b*, 9. These two sources were put together by an able Christian writer, who by a series of additions and changes brought it into its present form. Although Weiss' theory is rejected on most hands as it stands, his work is full of fine suggestions, and many of these are of permanent value. I might instance one. This is, that originally instead of the seven trumpets there were three woes ; for, as Weiss has pointed out, the first four trumpets are not only repetitions of what is found elsewhere in the book, but are also feebler and wholly conventional repetitions. My own study of the

5

first four trumpets led me independently to
this conclusion, and mainly on other grounds.
Their diction is against their originality.
Like earlier critics, he points out that xi. 14
followed originally on ix. 21. This verse runs :
"The second woe is past : behold the third
woe cometh soon." But the second woe closed
with ix. 21. He also draws attention to the
obvious fact that in xxi. 1–8 and in xxi. 9–
xxii. 5, the Heavenly Jerusalem is twice
described and in different terms.

The last eminent scholar, whose work calls
for treatment here, as a representative of the
Redaction Hypothesis, and who is a believer in
a Jewish background of the Apocalypse, is
Von Soden. While J. Weiss is often hesitating
and tentative in his statements, Von Soden
hardly ever entertains a doubt. His hypothesis (*The Books of the New Testament*, translated 1907, pp. 338–374) is as follows. Nearly
three-fourths of the Apocalypse are derived
from a Jewish apocalypse, beginning with vi.
12–17 and ending with xxii. 5. From these
chapters, of course, he is obliged to delete
frequent Christian clauses and verses, either
as deliberate insertions of the first editor or of
the second (for he assumes a double redaction), or as marginal glosses subsequently incorporated into the text. With regard to the

Jewish Apocalypse, he holds that the simplest hypothesis is to accept it as already existing as a whole : though not quite homogeneous, it exhibits, in his opinion, a wonderful consistency in the development of events, and he declares it to be "the most precious jewel in the glittering necklace of Jewish Apocalypses," and states that it was written between May and August of the year 70 A.D. Twenty years later this book fell into the hands of John, whose devoted adhesion to the faith of Christ involved him in banishment to Patmos. Seeing that the high hopes of the Jewish Apocalypse had not been fulfilled, he re-edited it from a Christian standpoint—prefixing the Seven Letters and the Seven Seals, interpolating certain clauses and verses into the Jewish Apocalypse, and making certain additions in the closing chapter. The book was finally edited by another writer, who added the opening and closing verses i. 1–3 and xxii. 18–20.

This theory of Von Soden is, in my opinion, just as untenable as those of Vischer, Kohler and Weiss, and not half so suggestive as that of the last scholar. And yet there is some truth at the base of all these theories. Jewish elements have been incorporated into the text, but they constitute only a small proportion of the text—not three-fourths or four-fifths of it, as some of these writers would have us believe ; and they do not form the foundation of the book, which is essentially Christian, but only certain portions of the superstructure ; and in their new setting they are given, in almost every instance, a new connotation and meaning distinct from what they originally bore.

None of the above theories have gained the assent of scholars, but some of them have made permanent contributions to our knowledge of our author.

ii. *Sources Hypothesis.* — This hypothesis, which has in part been already noticed, was advocated by Weyland, Spitta, Schmidt and Briggs. It assumes the existence of two, three or more independent sources, which were subsequently put together by a redactor.

With Weyland we have already dealt (see p. 62). We must take account of Spitta and Briggs. Spitta's work (*Offenbarung des Johannes*), published in 1889, is the most thoroughgoing and detailed criticism that exists on the subject, but it is artificial and unconvincing in its main lines. First of all, Spitta assumes a primitive Christian Apocalypse, written soon after 60 A.D., con- sisting of i. 4–6, 9–19, ii.–vi., viii. 1, vii. 9–17. Here, in divergence from Völter, Vischer and

Weyland, he assigns the Seven Letters to the original Apocalypist, and chaps. iv.–vi. and ii.–iii. to the same author. So far his criticism is, we hold, wholly justifiable. But the rest is untenable in the main. He discovers two Jewish sources,—one, a Trumpet Source, written in the reign of Caligula, and the other a Bowl Source, written in the time of Pompey. All three sources were put together by a Christian redactor in the time of Trajan.

Dr. Briggs' theory (*The Messiah of the Apostles*, 1895, pp. 284–437), to which we now turn, is the most complex that has yet been propounded.

There were originally six independent apocalypses and four different redactions. The first redaction dealt with the Seals, the Trumpets and the Bowls; the second prefixed to this work the Letters to the Seven Churches; the third added the two independent apocalypses on the Beast and the Dragon; while the fourth and last re-edited the third with many additions throughout.

I have a great admiration for Dr. Briggs' breadth of scholarship and great versatility, but it is hard to take his theory seriously. It is open in an overwhelming degree to every objection that can be brought against the use of the Sources Hypothesis. Moreover, like all the works classed under this heading, it breaks down hopelessly in the face of the general linguistic unity of the book, which the Philological Method has already in part brought to light.

In fact, what is now needed is a further development of his Philological Method, or, in other words, a more exact study of the style, the vocabulary and the grammar of the Apocalyptist. So far as the grammar goes, the book is absolutely unique in all Greek literature. It is true, indeed, that Bousset has given special attention to the study of the grammar, and his contribution in this respect is deserving of high praise. But it has failed to take account of many of the most characteristic features of the book. To some of these, which it has been my good fortune to discover, I will draw attention later. In the meantime, I will here give a few characteristic constructions that belong to the book as a whole, most of which have already been recognised.

The numerals, as a rule, follow after their noun, unless preceded by the article. Thus δέκα is always postpositive except in xvii. 12, where a source is used. ἑπτά is likewise postpositive : in a few cases, where it is prepositive, the passages are suspicious on other grounds. πέντε and ἕξ are postpositive, whereas τέσσαρες is prepositive and δύο either.

Again, the phrase "inhabitants of the earth," which is of frequent occurrence, always has the form οἱ κατοικοῦντες τὴν γῆν except in two verses, which on other grounds come from another hand. Still more remarkable is our author's extraordinary use of the very frequent phrase "he that sitteth on the throne." When it is in the nominative or accusative, ὁ καθήμενος or τὸν καθήμενον is always followed by ἐπὶ τὸν θρόνον. But if it is in the genitive, then the form is τοῦ καθημένου ἐπὶ τοῦ θρόνου, and if in the dative, τῷ καθημένῳ ἐπὶ τῷ θρόνῳ. Again, the phrase "on their foreheads" is either ἐπὶ τὸν μέτωπον αὐτῶν or ἐπὶ τῶν μετώπων αὐτῶν.

Finally, Hebraisms are to be found everywhere. Indeed, it would be possible to devote several chapters to the Hebraisms and the peculiar late Greek, and non-Greek constructions that characterise, not one-fourth, or one-third of the Apocalypse as against the rest, but that characterise the Apocalypse from its beginning to its close. In fact, it exhibits a marvellous unity of style *as a whole*, and this unity is manifested not in normal constructions, but in abnormal. I emphasise the words *as a whole*; for not a few passages betray signs of another hand, or of sources whether Hebrew or Greek. It is on the ground of this general unity of style in diction and construction that we are obliged to reject all such violent hypotheses as those of Spitta, Vischer, J. Weiss, Von Soden and the like. The problem of the Apocalypse cannot be solved either by the Redaction Hypothesis, or by the Sources Hypothesis, or by a combination of the two. Notwithstanding, these two schools have brought many invaluable facts to light. They have shown incontrovertibly that within the Apocalypse there are certain verses, passages and sections which are inconsistent with the tone and character of the whole. In order, therefore, to account for a general unity of plan and diction, and the no less assured existence of certain verses and sections at variance with their adjoining contexts and the tone of the entire work, we must have recourse to the third hypothesis—the Fragment Hypothesis.

iii. *The Fragment Hypothesis.*—To Weizsäcker we owe the first statement of this theory in his suggestion that, while the book is a unity, the author made free use of other materials. These in the first and second editions of his *Apostolic Age* (1886 and 1892) he specifies as vii. 1–8, xi. 1–13, xii.–xiii., xvii. This view has been further worked out by Sabatier (*Les origines littéraires de l'apoc. de St. Jean*, 1888), Schoen, and Bousset, and adopted by Porter in America and by Scott and Moffatt in this country.[1]

The labours of these scholars show that, while the book is the production of one author, all its parts are not of the same date, nor are they one and all his first-hand creation—in fact, they have made the assumption of an *absolute* unity in the details of the Apocalypse a practical impossibility. Incongruities are brought to light not only between certain sections and the main scheme of the book, but between these and their immediate contexts. These sections are vii. 1–8, xi. 1–13, xii., xiii., xvii., xviii., xx., xxi. 9–xxii. 5.

We shall for a moment pause on vii. 1–8, the sealing of the 144,000 from the twelve tribes of Israel. This is probably a fragment of a Jewish-Christian Apocalypse, or a recast of a Jewish Apocalypse. First of all, it is strongly particularistic : it limits the elect of God to these Jewish Christians. Observe that Judah is placed first, as we find in the Christian interpolations in the Testaments of the XII Patriarchs. This is against all the O.T. lists, unless where geographical or like considerations intervene. No Jew after 250 B.C., unless he had become a Christian, would have placed

---

[1] Bruston's work, *Les origines de l'apocalypse*, 1888, comes under this hypothesis, according to Bousset.

Judah before Levi. Its independent origin
has been inferred also by Spitta and subsequent
scholars, from the fact that the four winds,
which in vii. 1 are said to be held fast, lest
they should break in elemental fury on land
and sea, are not let loose nor referred to in
the subsequent narrative.

Thus these verses belong to some original
Jewish-Christian writing, and each of the above
statements had a natural meaning in its original
context. But in their present context they
have lost their original meaning. The sealing
means to the original writer preservation from
physical evils and death; but it cannot bear
this meaning in the Apocalypse. What it
does mean we shall investigate further on.

I have given this one instance of the critical
method of dealing with the text. Time will
not admit of any such further detailed examination. But certain of the above sections,
which are really foreign to the context, cannot
be explained from any Literary-Critical method.
These are found in chaps. xi., xii., xiii., xvii.
The symbols and myths which appear in
these chapters are not the creation of the
writer, but are borrowed from tradition, and
that a tradition not always necessarily Jewish.
In some instances the materials are too foreign
to his subject to lend themselves to his purpose

without the help of violent expedients. For the elucidation of these foreign elements a new method—the Traditional-Historical—is necessary, a method which we owe to the brilliant scholar Gunkel.

§ 17. *Traditional-Historical Method.*

Gunkel in his work, *Schöpfung und Chaos* (1895), opened up new lines of investigation. He shows that tradition largely fixes the forms of figures and symbols in Apocalyptic. Each new apocalypse is to some extent a reinterpretation of traditional material, which the writer uses not wholly freely, but with reverence, from the conviction that it contained the key to the mysteries of the present and the future. On the other hand, since much of the material of an apocalypse is reinterpreted tradition, it is necessary to distinguish between its original meaning and the new turn given to it in the Apocalypse. Occasionally details in the transmitted material are unintelligible even to our author, and in these cases he omits any reference to them in his interpretation. The presence of such details is strong evidence of the writer's use of foreign material.

§ 18. *Religious-Historical Method.*

Together with the *Traditional-Historical,*

Gunkel combines the *Religious-Historical*. From the fact that a certain statement or doctrine in the Apocalypse is not Christian, we cannot forthwith conclude to its Jewish origin. Materials from other religions, whether Babylonian, Egyptian or Greek, are to be found in xii. and other chapters. These materials have, it is true, been more or less assimilated, but traces of their non-Christian and non-Jewish origin still survive.[1]

In dependence on the above methods the best modern commentary was published by Bousset in 1896, in which many fresh contributions were made, and a second edition of this work in 1906. The same lines of interpretation are followed in the main by Pfleiderer in his second edition of his *Urchristenthum*, and by Holtzmann in the third edition of his Commentary, published five years ago with the assistance of W. Bauer. In our own country the above results have to a considerable extent been elaborated by Porter in Hastings' *Bible Dictionary* and *The Messages of the Apocalyptical Writers*, and popularised by Scott in a small commentary. Professor Sanday

[1] Valuable material will be found on these questions in Clemen's *Religionsgeschichtliche Erklärung des Neuen Testaments*, 1909—an English edition of which has recently been published by T. and T. Clark.

has published a short study in the *Journal of
Theological Studies*, and Moffatt an admirable
commentary in the *Expositor's Greek Testament*. By means of the work of the past
century, and particularly of the last fifteen years,
the Apocalypse has ceased to be the hopeless
riddle that the sanest and greatest scholars
of earlier centuries held it to be, and "has
quickly passed," as Holtzmann puts it, "into
the position of one of the most valuable
documents for the primitive age of the
Christian Church."

Notwithstanding, the land is not yet wholly
possessed. Some independent problems still
await fuller solution, and amongst them this :
Are the visions in the Apocalypse the genuine
results of spiritual experience, or are they
artificial products? Weizsäcker unhesitatingly
advocates the latter view. But the serious
students of later times cannot follow in his
footsteps. The writer's belief in his prophetic
office and his obvious conviction of the inviolable
sanctity of his message postulate the existence
of actual spiritual experiences behind his
visions, and the only difficulty lies in determin-
ing to what extent such experience does under-
lie the revelations of the Apocalypse.

In bringing this section of our studies to
a close, I may add that the author of this

great book has, despite the burden of an all
but overwhelming tradition and the use of
a style which sets every canon of correct
writing at defiance, but which nevertheless
observes laws of its own, bequeathed to mankind a κτῆμα ἐς ἀεί — an imperishable possession, the true worth of which lies in the
splendid energy of its faith, in the unfaltering
certainty that God's own cause is at issue now
and here and must ultimately prevail, and
that the cause of Jesus Christ is inseparably
linked therewith, and the main aim of which,
as is clear from every page, is to emphasise the
overwhelming worth of things spiritual as
contrasted with things material, and in the
next place to glorify martyrdom, to encourage
the faithful to face death with constancy, nay
more, with rapturous joy.

" Blessed are the dead that die in the Lord."

CHAPTER III.

THE HEBRAIC STYLE OF THE APOCALYPSE.

The abnormal type of the Greek of the Apocalypse has been recently said to be characteristic of the vernacular Greek of this period, and the existence of Hebraisms strictly so called denied. These positions are untenable. The style of the Apocalypse is absolutely unique in all Greek literature, while linguistically it is more Hebraic than the Septuagint.

THE Hebraic style of the Apocalypse has always been freely acknowledged till the present generation. But owing to the researches of Thumb, Deissmann and Moulton, who have succeeded in bringing to light such a mass of fresh knowledge on the vernacular Greek which prevailed before and after the Christian era, a new attitude on this question has been assumed by all scholars in some degree and by some scholars in a most extravagant degree. Thus, to take one of the latter school, Professor Moulton (*Gramm. of N.T. Greek*[1], p. 8 sq.) affirms that

" even the Greek of the Apocalypse itself does not seem to owe any of its blunders to Hebraism. The author's uncertain use of cases is obvious to the most casual reader. . . . We find him perpetually indifferent to concord. But the less educated papyri give us plentiful parallels from a field whose Semitism cannot be suspected. . . . Apart from places where he may be definitely translating a Semitic document, there is no reason to believe that his grammar would have been materially different had he been a native of Oxyrhynchus, assuming the extent of Greek education the same."

This is without doubt an extreme statement of the case, and Professor Swete (*Apocalypse*[2], ii. p. cxxiv, note) rightly rejoins : that " it is precarious to compare a *literary*[1] document with a collection of personal and business letters, accounts, and other ephemeral writings ; slips in word-formation or in syntax, which are to be expected in the latter, are phenomenal in the former, and if they find a place there, *can only be attributed to life-long habits of thought*.[1]   Moreover, it remains to be considered how far the quasi-Semitic colloquialisms of the papyri are themselves due to the influence of the large Greek-speaking Jewish population of the Delta."

[1] The italics are due to the present writer.

My own studies, which have extended over more than 2000 years of Greek literature, and have concerned themselves specially with Hellenistic Greek, so far as this Greek was used as a vehicle of Jewish thought, have led me to adopt a very different conclusion on this question, and this is, that *the linguistic character of the Apocalypse is absolutely unique.*

Its language differs from that of the LXX and the other versions of the Old Testament, from the Greek of the Apocrypha and Pseudepigrapha, and from that of the Papyri. Of course, it has points in common with all these phases of later Greek, but nevertheless it possesses a very distinct character of its own. No literary document of the Greek world exhibits such a vast multitude of solecisms. It would almost seem that the author of the Apocalypse deliberately set at defiance the grammarian and the ordinary rules of syntax. That he has done so successfully is unquestionable. But it appears to me that such a description would do him injustice. He had no such intention. He is full of his subject, and like the great Hebrew prophets of old is a true artist. His object is to drive home his message with all the powers at his command, and this he does in some of the sublimest passages in all literature. Naturally with such an object in view he has

6

no thought of consistently breaking any rule
of syntax. How, then, are we to explain the
unbridled licence of his Greek constructions?
The reason clearly is that, while he writes in
Greek, he thinks in Hebrew, and the thought
has naturally affected the vehicle of expression.
But this is not all. He never mastered Greek
idiomatically—even the Greek of his own
period. To him very many of its particles
were apparently unknown, and the multi-
tudinous shades of meaning which they ex-
pressed in the various combinations into which
they entered, were never grasped at all, or only
in a very inadequate degree.

In fact, the language of his adoption was not
for him a normalised and rigid medium of
utterance—nay rather, it was still in a fluent
condition, and so he used it freely, remodelling
its syntactical forms and launching forth into
unusual or unheard of expressions with a view
to the better setting forth of his ideas; and that
he achieved his end, even the most fastidious of
Greek scholars must admit, so far as they suc-
ceed in understanding his work. For in its own
literature the book stands absolutely without
a rival, while in the literature of all time it has
deservedly won for itself a place in the van.

One obvious result of the inherent greatness
and sublimity of the work, despite the sole-

cistic character of its form, is that perhaps no book in any literature suffers so little by translation; for of necessity the bulk of its irregularities in syntax must vanish in the process of translation, while its essential greatness alike in thought and expression remains. But this, again, is attended by an unavoidable drawback for the non-Greek reader; for in the process of translation the bulk of the idiosyncrasies of style, which differentiate this book from all other Jewish and Christian works, and especially from the Fourth Gospel, must inevitably disappear.

I must now justify the general statements which have just been made, though, of course, only a very small part of the evidence can be put forward on the present occasion.

Even this evidence will, I hope, be sufficient to produce a conviction that the style is Hebraic in character. If time and opportunity permitted, it would be easy to prove that the style of the Apocalypse is more Hebraic than that of the LXX.

Hebraisms in the Greek text of the Apocalypse, to some of which exceptional parallels can be found in vernacular Greek but not to others.

1. First of all, it might be recognised as a

rule that our author follows the Hebrew idiom according to which the word or phrase, which stands in apposition to a noun in an oblique case, is put in the nominative. Such solecisms are found occasionally in the LXX, but what is a rare phenomenon in this Greek version of the Old Testament is actually a recognised idiom in the Greek text of the Apocalypse. Our author has, in fact, adopted a Hebrew idiom into his Greek, and naturalised it there, as in i. 5, ii. 13, 20, iii. 12, vii. 4, viii. 9, ix. 14, xiv. 12, 14. He does not, it is true, always abandon the legitimate Greek construction in such cases, but he does so sufficiently often to legitimate our recognition of it as a marked characteristic of his style.

Of the above passages I must quote two or three. Thus in i. 5 we have ἀπὸ Ἰησοῦ Χριστοῦ ὁ μάρτυς ὁ πιστός instead of ἀπὸ Ἰ. Χ. τοῦ μάρτυρος τοῦ πιστοῦ = " from Jesus Christ the faithful witness." In ii. 20 we have ἀφεῖς τὴν γυναῖκα Ἰεζάβελ, ἡ λέγουσα ἑαυτὴν προφῆτιν, instead of τὴν λέγουσαν ἑαυτὴν προφῆτιν = "thou sufferest the woman Jezebel which calleth herself a prophetess." Again, in iii. 12, τὸ ὄνομα τῆς πόλεως . . . ἡ καταβαίνουσα ἐκ τοῦ οὐρανοῦ = "the name of the city . . . which cometh down from heaven." Now that a Jew could naturally and unwittingly fall

into this solecism, when using an inflected
language other than his own, is illustrated by
Professor Nestle (*Textual Criticism of the Greek
Testament*, p. 330 n.), who quotes the following
gem from Salomon Bär in his translation of the
Massoretic note at the end of the Books of
Samuel (Leipzig, 1892, p. 158), "ad mortem
Davidis *rex* Israelis." This is a perfect illus-
tration of what occurs frequently in our text.
The same solecism occurs in the Greek translation of the Old Testament. Cf. Ezek. xxiii.
12 (τοὺς υἱοὺς τῶν Ἀσσυρίων . . . ἱππεῖς ἱππαζόμενοι
ἐφ᾿ ἵππων—A).

2. Next, a noticeable Hebraism is the indeclinable use of λέγων or λέγοντες = the Hebrew
לֵאמֹר. Thus in v. 11 we have φωνὴν ἀγγέλων
. . . λέγοντες instead of λέγουσαν or λεγόντων.

Again, in xiv. 6 sq. there is an extraordinary
instance of this usage, where the phrase ἄλλον
ἄγγελον is followed by three participles depend-
ing upon it, the first two of which (πετόμενον
and ἔχοντα) are rightly in the accusative, but
the third (λέγων) is in the nominative ; in other
words, the indeclinable use of λέγων. Other
instances occur in iv. 1, xi. 1, 15, xix. 6
(Westcott and Hort, margin). This solecism,
owing to the Hebrew background, occurs in the
LXX; cf. Gen. xv. 1, xxii. 20, xxxviii. 13, xlv.
16, xlviii. 20, etc.).

3. Next, there is the *nominativus pendens*, iii. 12, ὁ νικῶν, ποιήσω αὐτόν ; in vi. 8, ὁ καθήμενος ἐπάνω αὐτοῦ, ὄνομα αὐτῷ ὁ θάνατος—a very frequent construction in Hebrew, and not unattested in the rest of the N.T. (cf. Blass, *Gram. N.T. Greek*, Eng. trans., 283).

4. The oblique forms of the personal pronoun are added pleonastically, as in Hebrew, to relatives : iii. 8 (ἣν οὐδεὶς δύναται κλεῖσαι αὐτήν) xii. 6, 14, xiii. 8, or to participles ii. 7 (τῷ νικῶντι δώσω αὐτῷ), iii. 12, vi. 4.

That exceptionally such idioms are found in the vernacular Greek, and in a few cases in classical Greek, does not make against the fact that they are here due to Semitic influence ; since, as the rest of the evidence proves, our text is more Semitic in character than the bulk of the LXX.

5. The absence of the use of the instrumental dative, the place of which is supplied by ἐν. This usage is to be met with in vernacular Greek also. It belongs, nevertheless, to the Hebraic colouring of our text.

6. Another Semiticism in our author's style is his use of the participle as a finite verb. This usage is fairly frequent in Hebrew, while in Aramaic it is practically the normal usage.

It is quite true that in late vernacular

Greek this usage is attested in a few instances (see Moulton, *Gram.*[1] 223). Moulton also recognises its existence in Rom. v. 11, xii. 6 ; Heb. viii. 10, x. 16 ; and Blass in 2 Cor. v. 12, vii. 5.

While we grant the occurrence of this vernacular idiom in these cases, it does not do away with the fact that, when the participle is used as a finite verb in a manifestly Hebraic Greek text such as that of the Apocalypse, it is to be regarded as a Hebraism. As such, therefore, we regard ἔχων in x. 2 and xxi. 12, 14, and also in xii. 2, which should be translated : "And she was with child, and cried in her travail and pain to be delivered" (= וְהִיא הָרָה וַתִּזְעַק חוֹכָה וּמְחַבְּלָה [1] לָלֶדֶת). The author being accustomed to the use of the participle as a finite verb in his native idiom, transfers this usage into the language of his adoption.

The evidence so far appears sufficient to prove the Hebraic character of the text. It is true that to most of the individual idioms analogous uses may be found exceptionally in vernacular Greek, but that such an accumulation of exceptions should be brought together

[1] These two participles are found together in Ps. vii. 15. If the retroversion is right, possibly מחבלה is corrupt for מיחלה = "hoping." In that case we should have "cried out, being in travail and hoping to be delivered."

within such narrow compass in a literary
work must appear incredible to a sound judgment.

*Other and still stronger grounds for the
Hebraic or Semitic character of the text.*

1. All but universally our author uses not
the LXX but the Hebrew text of the Old
Testament.

2. The order and structure of his language
is thoroughly Hebraic. Thus, with the exception of a section or two, which on quite distinct
grounds we conclude were borrowed from other
sources, the verb as a rule comes first, then the
subject, and next the object. This Hebraic order
of the sentence is wholly abandoned for the
normal Greek order in chap. xi.

3. The parallelism of the style is too obvious
to be ignored. The author repeatedly breaks
forth into verse in which the parallelism of
Hebrew poetry is carefully observed.

Large sections of the book were written in
stanzas of three or four lines each. Their
structure is so clear that by means of it we can
at times detect glosses. Thus, to take an
example, it is possible to recover the original
form of the vision in iv. 2–8, which appears to
have been composed of four stanzas of four lines
each and to have read as follows:

I.

2 And behold there was a throne set in heaven,
And on the throne was one seated,
3 And he that sat was to look upon like a jasper stone
and a sardius,
And (there was) a rainbow round about the throne
like an emerald to look upon.

II.

5 And out of the throne proceeded lightnings and
voices and thunders :
6 And before the throne there was as it were a glassy
sea like unto crystal,
And round about the throne were four living
creatures,
Full of eyes before and behind.

III.

7 And the first creature was like a lion,
And the second creature was like an ox,
And the third creature had a face as of a man,
And the fourth creature was like a flying eagle.

IV.

8 And the four creatures had each six wings,
And they rested not day and night singing :
Holy, holy, holy, is the Lord God Almighty,
Which was, and which is, and which is to come.

4. The co-ordination of the participle in one
of the oblique cases and the finite verb, which
is not found, so far as I am aware, in any
form of true vernacular Greek, is in Hebrew
essentially an idiom, and that a common one.

In the New Testament outside the Apocalypse
it is attested at all events in 2 John 2, τὴν
ἀλήθειαν τὴν μένουσαν ἐν ἡμῖν καὶ μεθ' ἡμῶν ἔσται ;
Col. i. 26.[1] In these two passages the peculiar syntax, so far as I am aware, cannot be
explained from any eccentricity or blunder
in the vernacular Greek ; for in these we have
a dependent participle (in the accusative and
dependent on the article) resolved into an
indicative in the following sentence. Now,
as Driver (*Moods and Tenses*[3], 163) writes,
" it is a common custom with Hebrew writers,
after employing a participle, to change the construction, and, if they wish to subjoin other
verbs which logically should be participles . . .
to pass to the use of the finite verb." [2] We

---

[1] John i. 32 is not to be taken as instance of this idiom ;
see Abbott, *Johannine Gram.* p. 335.

A form of this idiom is found in 1 Cor. vii. 13, γυνὴ, ἥτις ἔχει
ἄνδρα ἄπιστον καὶ οὗτος συνευδοκεῖ, where the last three words
would in ordinary Greek be καὶ συνευδοκοῦντα, *i.e.* " a woman
who hath an husband unbelieving but content to dwell with
her." Here St. Paul's Greek would represent idiomatic Hebrew
(or והוא רצה) בעל בלתי מאמין ורצה. In Heb. viii. 10, x. 16, the
participle is not in the oblique case. Moreover, in these passages the Greek participle here either represents a participle in
the Hebrew where a finite verb stands now in the Massoretic, or
it is used as the finite verb, as occasionally in the vernacular
Greek.

[2] In the present instance I am limiting our consideration to
the co-ordination of the participle in an oblique case and the
finite verb, in order to avoid the possibility of an explanation
of this idiom from vernacular Greek.

have here the natural explanation of these two
passages so far as the syntax goes, and if this
is so, as I am convinced it is, the rendering
of the Authorised Version is right in both and
the Revised Version wrong. So far for this
usage outside the Apocalypse. But now, turning to the Apocalypse, what do we find there?
Is this idiom an isolated one? By no means.
It occurs seven times, and is relatively of far
more frequent occurrence than in the LXX;
for the LXX appears only occasionally to repro-
duce this idiom literally. We might compare
Isa. v. 8, 23, Ezek. xxii. 3, where the Hebrew
is translated into idiomatic Greek, while in
Gen. xxvii. 33, Isa. xiv. 17, the Hebrew idiom
is reproduced in the Greek.

In the Apocalypse, on the other hand, it
emerges in the first chapter in vers. 5, 6; and
four times in the chapters that follow, *i.e.* in
ii. 2, 9, 20, vii. 14.[1] In every one of these
passages the Revised Version rendering is
wrong and that of the Authorised Version right,

[1] It is not improbable that in iii. 7 we have a Hebraism
repeated twice : τάδε λέγει ὁ ἅγιος . . . ὁ ἀνοίγων καὶ οὐδεὶς
κλείει καὶ κλείων καὶ οὐδεὶς ἀνοίγει. Here the Greek can be
retranslated literally into Hebrew, but whereas it is Hebrew
idiom, הפתח ואין סגר והסגר ואין פתח, it cannot be said to be
Greek. The sense of the Greek is, "Who openeth so that no
one closeth, and closeth so that no one openeth" (ὁ ἀνοίγων
ὥστε μηδένα κλείειν καὶ κλείων ὥστε μηδένα ἀνοίγειν).

save in one where its text is untenable.   The
latter, perhaps through following the ancient
versions—the Syriac and Latin—consciously
or unconsciously reproduced correctly the
Hebrew idiom underlying the Greek.   Let me
give examples.   In i. 5, 6 the Greek runs :
τῷ ἀγαπῶντι (A.V. ἀγαπήσαντι) ἡμᾶς καὶ λύσαντι
ἡμᾶς ἐκ τῶν ἁμαρτιῶν ἡμῶν ἐν τῷ αἵματι αὐτοῦ, καὶ
ἐποίησεν ἡμᾶς βασιλείαν (A.V. βασιλεῖς).

This the Authorised Version renders : " Unto
him that loved us . . . and hath made us
kings" : and rightly, for it has treated the finite
verb exactly as if it were a participle, according
to the Hebrew idiom.   Let us now turn to the
Revised Version.   Its reading is : " Unto him
that loveth us . . . and he made us to be a
kingdom."   Our first criticism of this rendering is that it is not English.   The phrase,
" Unto him that loveth us," stands without
any grammatical connection with the rest of
the sentence.   In the next place, it is not a
translation of the text, as we have already
recognised.   If anything is to be supplied
before " made," it should be " that " and not
" he."   " Unto him that loveth us . . . and
that made," etc.   Next, in ii. 2 the Greek τοὺς
λέγοντας ἑαυτοὺς ἀποστόλους καὶ οὐκ εἰσίν is
rightly rendered by the Authorised Version,
" which say they are apostles and are not."

Here again the Revised Version wrongly
renders, "which call themselves apostles and
they are not." The same construction recurs
in ii. 9, where the Authorised Version is again
right and the Revised Version wrong. The
next instance in ii. 20 is very obvious : τὴν
γυναῖκα Ἰεζάβελ, ἡ λέγουσα ἑαυτὴν προφῆτιν καὶ
διδάσκει. Here, just as in the preceding cases,
the verb διδάσκει, "teaches," ought to be a
participle in idiomatic Greek, but the writer
has reproduced his own Hebrew idiom literally.
The text of the Authorised Version is here
very corrupt, and accordingly its rendering
is not available. As regards the Revised
Version, the text it followed is the best, but its
rendering is just as incorrect as elsewhere.
Instead, therefore, of translating " which calleth
herself a prophetess and she teacheth," with
the Revised Version, we should translate " which
calleth herself a prophetess and teacheth,"
as if it were ἡ λέγουσα . . . καὶ διδάσκουσα.

There is one more instance of this idiom,
but the participle is not in an oblique case, i.e.
in vii. 14 : οἱ ἐρχόμενοι ἐκ τῆς θλίψεως τῆς μεγάλης
καὶ ἔπλυναν τὰς στολὰς αὐτῶν.

Here the finite verb ἔπλυναν is co-ordinated
with the participle ἐρχόμενοι, and should be
translated as if it were a participle dependent
on the article. Accordingly the text is to be

rendered : "These are they who came out of the great tribulation and washed their robes." The Authorised Version is here on the whole right, but the Revised Version has again mis-rendered this idiom as follows : " These are they which came out of the great tribulation, and they washed their robes."

From these criticisms it is not to be inferred that the Revised Version is elsewhere inferior to the Authorised Version in accuracy.   This, of course, is not the case.   The above misrender-ings are due to the Revisers treating the Apoca-lypse as if it were firstly and lastly a Greek book written by a Greek.   This particular Hebraism in the Apocalypse has not, so far as I am aware, ever been recognised heretofore.

5.   There are pure Hebraisms in the text to which no analogy can be found in the vernacular Greek.   I will adduce only three. In xvii. 8 there is the use of the singular ὄνομα, "name," instead of the plural ὀνόματα, "names," where all the multitude of the lost is referred to, is a Hebrew idiom.   Hence we must render, "they whose names have not been written in the book of life," not "they whose name," as in the Revised Version ; for this is not English, any more than it was Greek.   Next, in xii. 5 we have the extraordinary statement, "she was delivered of a son, a man child" (or "a male").

Now neither in Greek nor English can a son be anything but a man child. To add such a clause after the term " son " would be absurd. But this is not so in Hebrew. The plural בנים (= "sons") means occasionally "male and female children" (Gen. iii. 16 ; Exod. xxi. 5, xxii. 23). Hence in Josh. xvii. 2 we have the expression " the sons of Manasses, the males " (בני מנשה הזכרים), and in Jer. xx. 15, " A son, a male (or 'man child'—בן זכר) is born to thee." In this last passage we have exactly the same expression as in our text.

The third pure Hebraism is the very remarkable use our author makes of ὡς, which he places before either the subject of the verb or its object with the meaning—" the likeness of." No attempt, so far as I am aware, has been made to explain this use. But its origin seems to me to be quite clear. It is not Greek, but it is used by our author as the equivalent of the Hebrew כְּ. In the LXX it is used in this wholly non-Greek sense as a translation of the Hebrew prefix (cf. Num. ix. 15 ; Dan. x. 18). Thus ὡς στέφανοι in ix. 7 of our text means " the likeness of crowns," or "what was like crowns"; in xix. 1, ὡς φωνὴν μεγάλην, " the likeness of a mighty voice." The English versions, " as it were crowns " and " as it were a mighty voice," will do for

purposes of translation, but they conceal the
origin of the idiom. This usage is very frequent in the Apocalypse. Possibly we have
here also the explanation of the solecism
ὅμοιον υἱὸν ἀνθρώπου, "like a son of man,"
which occurs twice in our text (i. 13, xiv. 14).
Now ὅμοιος is the equivalent of ὡς in this
sense, as we know from 1 Enoch xviii. 13
(ὡς ὄρη μεγάλα) compared with xxi. 3 (ὁμοίους
ὄρεσιν μεγάλοις). Hence it may here take the
same construction as ὡς; for ὡς does not affect
the case of the noun which it precedes.

*Passages in the Apocalypse that require to be
translated into Hebrew in order to be
understood.*

We have now come to the last class of evidence which I propose to lay before you in
favour of the Hebraic character of our text.
If this evidence is valid, it is the strongest
that can be advanced. In the course of my
study of the text of the Apocalypse, I have
come to the conclusion that not only does the
author think in Hebrew, but that occasionally
he also translates already existing Hebrew documents into Greek. We have already had good
grounds for the former conclusion in the
evidence just brought before you. I will now
further substantiate this evidence by a study

of the remarkable passage in x. 1, where it reads as follows : " And I saw another strong angel coming down out of heaven, arrayed with a cloud : and a rainbow was upon his head, and his face was as the sun, and his feet as pillars of fire." Now all this verse is perfectly clear save the last clause—οἱ πόδες αὐτοῦ ὡς στύλοι πυρός = " his feet were like pillars of fire." Who ever heard such an extraordinary simile ? Feet like pillars of fire ! There must be some error here, and yet no scholar has hitherto called attention to it. The mistake, if there is a mistake, must lie either in πόδες = " feet " or στύλοι = " pillars." Now, whereas I can discover no corruption underlying στύλοι, it is not difficult to see how the term πόδες came to be placed here. The expression in Cant. v. 15, " his legs were like pillars of marble," supplies in fact the idea that should stand here. The Hebrew word רגל, which normally means " foot," has also the meaning of " leg " in 1 Sam. xvii. 6 ;[1] Deut. xxviii. 57 ;[2] Isa. vii. 20. It is so rendered by the LXX in Ezek. i. 7, xvi. 25. A derivative of this word is rendered by τὰ σκέλη in Dan. x. 6, by Theodotion.

Furthermore, in Palestinian Aramaic it is

---

[1] So, rightly, LXX, Pesh. and Vulg.
[2] So, rightly, LXX and Vulg.

used as meaning the "thigh" of an animal,
being a translation of כְּרָעַיִם; cf. Exod. xxix.
17; Lev. i. 13, viii. 21, ix. 14.   In Arabic this
word means either "foot or "leg."   From
these facts we see that, while our author had
in his mind the word רגל, he attached to it not
its ordinary meaning "foot," but its less usual
one " leg," and that he transferred this secondary meaning of the Hebrew word to its Greek
equivalent. It might appear at first sight that
he was wholly unjustified in supposing that
the primary and secondary meanings of the
Hebrew word, *i.e.* "foot" and "leg," belonged
also to the Greek word; and yet it is possible
that this secondary meaning of πούς (when used
as a rendering of the Hebrew) was not un-
exampled at the time.   For in the LXX it
appears as an equivalent of כרעים, "thigh," as
we have already observed in Ex. xxix. 17;
Lev. i. 9, 13, viii. 21, ix. 14.

From the above evidence we conclude that
we should render the clause in the Apocalypse:
"His legs were like pillars of fire." [1]

The next passage seems to postulate an
actual Hebrew background. In ii. 22 it is
said of the woman Jezebel: "Behold, I cast her

---

[1] In Dan. x. 6 the rendering should most probably follow
that of Theodotion : "his arms and his legs were like in colour
to burnished brass."

into a bed, and them that commit adultery with her into great tribulation." Now, how are we to explain the punishment that is designed by these words : "Behold, I cast her into a bed"? Ramsay and Moulton take the word κλίνη here to denote a banqueting couch ; but that this is wrong, will be seen as we proceed. The κλίνη is a bed of sickness or suffering, following as the due meed of her licentious teaching.

This interpretation has been rightly put forward by several scholars ; but, so far as I know, they have not explained how it can be justified. Now, if we retranslate it into Hebrew, we recognise that we have here a Hebrew idiom. In Hebrew (נפל למשכב), "to fall upon a bed" means "to take to one's bed," *i.e.* to become ill (cf. Ex. xxi. 18); and "to cast upon a bed" means "to cast upon a bed of illness." This idiom is found in 1 Macc. i. 5, vi. 8 (ἔπεσε ἐπὶ τὴν κοίτην), and Jud. viii. 3 (ἔπεσε ἐπὶ τὴν κλίνην), which books are translated from the Hebrew. Thus, if we wish to give the passage its true significance, we should read :

"Behold, I cast her on a bed of illness (or 'suffering')
And those who commit adultery with her into great
tribulation."[1]

הנני מפיל אתה למשכב[1]
ואת המנאפים אתה בצרה גדלה.

I will take only one passage more, *i.e.* xiii. 11.
In this passage we shall go still further than
we have gone before. Heretofore we have
considered cases in which difficulties arose,
owing to the fact that our author was con-
struing his Hebrew thought and diction into
Greek. In this passage, and it does not stand
alone, we have a piece of Greek which seems
not to admit of explanation, except on the
hypothesis that it is a translation from the
Hebrew, and that the Hebrew was corrupt.
Other passages in the chapter postulate the
same hypothesis. The passage immediately
before us is as follows :—

> "And I saw another beast coming up out of the earth,
>   And he had two horns like unto a lamb ;
>   And he spake as a dragon."

Now we may at once premise that the generally accepted and indeed the right interpretation of this second beast is that it represented
the heathen priesthood in Asia Minor, which
had for its office the worship of the Roman
Emperor. In the next place, it has been conjectured by several scholars that the text of
this chapter presupposes a Hebrew original.
My own studies have led me to the same
conclusion. Let us turn, now, to the passage
before us. The second line, *i.e.* "he had two
horns like unto a lamb," may be suggested—

at all events it is illustrated—by Matt. vii.
15 : " Beware of false prophets, which come to
you in sheep's clothing, but inwardly are raven-
ing wolves." The words therefore indicate the
mild appearance of the second beast : he had
two horns like unto a lamb. But what is to be
made of the clause that follows, " and he spake
as a dragon " ? There are no means of explaining it. A dragon does not speak. Is the
passage hopeless then ? By no means, in my
opinion, as I feel confident we can reconstruct
the text by translation into Hebrew. Thus
καὶ ἐλάλει ὡς δράκων = ‏ותדבר כתנין‎. Here, first of
all, the translator should have read the last
word of the unpointed Hebrew as ‏כַּתַּנִּין‎ = " as
the dragon," i.e. Satan, and not as ‏כְּתַנִּין‎, " as a
dragon," which is meaningless. Next, ‏תדבר‎ is
corrupt for ‏תאבד‎, exactly as in 2 Chron. xxii. 10,
where the Hebrew wrongly reads, " Athaliah spake with all the seed royal," instead
of " Athaliah slew all the seed royal," as in
2 Kings xi. 1.

A corruption that has crept into the Canonical text of the Old Testament might well
occur in the anonymous Hebrew document
behind chap. xiii. Hence instead of καὶ ἐλάλει,
" and he spake," we should read καὶ ἀπώλλυε
or καὶ ἦν ἀπολλύων = " and he was a destroyer,"
or " an apollyon." This phrase recalls the name

given to Satan in ix. 11, " his name in Hebrew is Abaddon, and in the Greek he hath the name Apollyon."

Satan was *the* Apollyon, but the second beast was *an* apollyon.

Thus the text read originally : " And he was a destroyer (or "apollyon) like the dragon." That he justified this title is seen in ver. 15, where it is stated that he caused all that did not worship the image of the first beast to be put to death.

To sum up, then, the entire verse is to be read as follows :

> " And I saw another beast coming up out of the earth,
> And he had two horns like a lamb ;
> But he was a destroyer like the dragon."

CHAPTER IV.

REVELATION VII.–IX.

It may seem strange that I have chosen to deal with chaps. vii.–ix. in this and the last lecture rather than with the first three or the fourth and fifth chapters, or such notable chapters as xii. and xiii. In all of these, it is quite true, there is still room for further investigation : but though the first three chapters, the fourth chapter and its immediate sequel, as well as the twelfth and thirteenth, have each important problems connected with them, their meaning is not *on the whole* difficult ; nor have they been so grossly misunderstood as chaps. vii.–ix. by practically the whole body of interpreters for the past 1600 years or more.

Chap. vii. has been misunderstood from the earliest centuries of the Christian era, and yet contains the key to the right interpretation of some of the immediately following chapters.

It is just because chap. vii. is one of the

most difficult chapters in the Apocalypse, and, if I am right, the chapter that has been most misunderstood, that I begin with it. And yet it is not only because it has been misunderstood that I do so, but because a right interpretation of this chapter is of vital importance, if we are to understand the main significance and the right sequence of thought in the next four chapters. To a certain extent this chapter contains the key to the orderly development of thought in the immediate chapters that follow in the Apocalypse. Naturally I cannot, in the course of two lectures, pretend to discuss all the difficulties that emerge in these three chapters, but I hope to remove the chief difficulties that stand in the way of our apprehending the writer's object and the orderly development of his thought in these chapters.

Contents of Chapter vii.

With this explanation I will now proceed to my task. The closing words of chap. vi., " The great day of his wrath is come, and who can abide it ? " lead us to expect immediately the opening of the seventh Seal, and therewith the advent of the day of wrath. Instead of this, however, we have a peaceful interlude. The march of events is checked, the four angels of destruction are bidden to stay their hand until the faithful should be sealed. The 144,000 Israelites are then sealed in vii. 4–8, and thereon follows, in the next nine verses, a vision of the martyrs in heaven. This vision is proleptic : that is, it is not what already exists in heaven that the Seer beholds, but what will exist presently, or at the end of the world. Nothing in the closing chapters of the Apocalypse surpasses in beauty and sublimity this blessed consummation of the martyrs, who come forth from the last great persecution which is about to fall upon the world.

In this chapter, then, we have two visions, and in them two main themes : one, the safe-guarding of the true Israel ; the other, the final blessedness of those who are to be martyred in the coming persecution.

Many critics assign vii. 1–8 and vii. 9–17 to different authors.

The real crux of this chapter is the signifi-cance and object of this sealing ; but we must first deal with the chapter as a whole, since, owing to the diverse character of the two visions, its integrity has been denied by many critics. Owing to the apparently Jewish, or Jewish-Christian, character of the vision of the sealing of the 144,000 Israelites in vii. 1–8, and the universalistic character of the second vision,

vii. 9–17, which embraces the faithful from all
mankind : that is, owing to the apparent par-
ticularism of the first section, and the un-
limited universalism of the second, most critics
have decided against the unity of the chapter.
Thus Spitta assigns vii. 1–8 to a Jewish Apocalypse, and makes vii. 9–17 the immediate sequel
of i.–vi.   On the other hand, Völter in his final
work on the subject, Vischer, Pfleiderer (1st
ed.), Schmidt, regard vii. 9–17 as an interpolation in what was originally a Jewish-
Christian or a Jewish work.   Others again
seek to reconstruct the original of this chapter
by making certain excisions.   Thus Erbes
removes vii. 4–8, 13–17 as additions from a
Jewish source ; while Weyland removes certain
phrases in vii. 9, 10, 14, 17 ; and Rauch deletes
vii. 13, 14 wholly, as well as certain phrases
in vii. 9, 10 as additions of a Christian writer.

*But the relative unity of the chapter is to be
maintained, and the two sections of the
chapter are to be taken as referring to
the same body of Christians, only under
different conditions.*

But a more excellent way of dealing with
the text is taken by Weizsäcker, Sabatier,
Schoen, Holtzmann, Bousset, Wellhausen,
Porter, Moffatt, who maintain the *relative*

unity of this chapter, and regard vii. 1–8
either as the work of our author, or as incorporated by him in the text, and adapted
thereto. Sabatier, Holtzmann, Hirscht, and
Bousset interpret the chapter as referring to
two different classes : vii. 1–8 as referring to
Jewish, and vii. 9–17 to Gentile Christians ;
while Reuss, Bovon, Schoen, Beyschlag, Porter,
Wellhausen, and Moffatt interpret the two
passages as describing the same body under
different conditions. My own studies have led
me independently and on different grounds
to somewhat the same conclusion. Thus,
though I shall be compelled to differ with
all interpreters for the last 1600 years as to
the significance of the sealing, I am glad to
find myself in agreement with such a large
body of scholars of the first rank, in holding
that the 144,000 that were sealed in vii. 4–8,
and the blessed company who stand clothed in
white raiment before the throne of God, are
one and the same, only under different conditions.

vii. 9–17 is from the hand of our Apocalyptist.

We must now proceed to discuss these
questions in detail, and first of all the relation
of vii. 9–17 to the rest of the Apocalypse. Now

an examination of the facts proves that this
section is from the hand of our Apocalyptist.
For (*a*) it proclaims the absolute universalism
of Christianity, as does the entire Apocalypse
so far as it comes from his hand; (*b*) in the
next place, its diction is clearly his. In these
nine verses the forms of diction are characteristic of our Apocalyptist : and in most of the
verses there is not only one such form, but
many. Let us take one verse as an example.
Thus in vii. 9 we have the verse opening with
the characteristic clause, μετὰ ταῦτα εἶδον καὶ ἰδού ;
next, the phrase ὄχλος πολύς, found in xix. 1, 6
in the same connection. Next, ἔθνους καὶ φυλῶν
καὶ λαῶν καὶ γλωσσῶν, " nation and tribes and
peoples and languages," which is found six
times elsewhere. Next, ἐνώπιον τοῦ θρόνου,
" before the throne," a frequent phrase in our
Apocalypse ; and the fuller form ἐνώπιον τοῦ
θρόνου καὶ ἐνώπιον τοῦ ἀρνίου recurs almost exactly
in xxii. 1, 3 ; and περιβεβλημένους στολὰς λευκάς
in vii. 9 (cf. vii. 13) is found in iii. 5, 18,
iv. 4.

It is clear that every phrase of this verse
comes from the hand of our Apocalyptist.
Now I have been applying the same rigorous
examination to every verse, and every clause,
and every phrase in the Apocalypse, and the
result of this examination furnishes irrefragable

proof that the main bulk of the book is from
the hand of one and the same author. This
does, however, not exclude the possibility
that here and there he has used sources,
Hebrew and Greek : that he has translated
the former, and in a few cases has taken over
the latter as they stand : or that he has adapted
to fresh contexts earlier visions of his own,
which in their original contexts had a somewhat different meaning.

*The Apocalypse consists of a whole body of
visions experienced at different times and
committed apparently on each occasion to
writing.*

Now, whilst I am touching on this question
of the relative unity of the book as a whole, it
would not be unfitting to emphasise the somewhat obvious fact that the Apocalypse cannot
be regarded as the outcome of a single vision
committed subsequently to writing. But
having done so we must go further : not only
were there many visions, but considerable
intervals of time must have elapsed between
them. A few were witnessed as early as
67 A.D., but the main body of the visions in
all probability belong to the period 92 and
95 A.D. Another point of importance in this
connection is, that the Seer was apparently

accustomed to commit his vision to writing immediately after its occurrence. Indeed, in these visions he frequently receives the command, "write down what thou hast seen," as in i. 11, 19, xiv. 13, xix. 9, xxi. 5. The Letters to the Seven Churches are dictated to him in the vision. On another occasion in x. 4, when the seven thunders utter their voices, the Seer at once prepared to write down what they said; but a voice from heaven forbade him, saying : "Seal up the utterances of the seven thunders, and do not write them" (x. 4). This last statement points to an interesting conclusion : in some of the visions the Seer was not in a trance, but in a conscious condition. This fact opens up important problems of vision, but we cannot deal with them here.

To return. From an examination of the diction of vii. 9–17 we are obliged to conclude that this section is from the hand of our Apocalyptist.

vii. 1–8 is derived, so far as the form goes, from our Apocalyptist.

Let us now turn to vii. 1–8 and discover, if we may, its origin. Now we find on examination that, so far as the diction is concerned, this section also comes from the hand of our Apocalyptist. Here we discern the importance of the linguistic evidence. These few verses exhibit clearly the style of our author, as most of the phraseology is his, and that also where it is most characteristic. Such evidence is conclusive against critics who would assign the section as it stands to quite a different author. But, though the *form* of the section is due to our author, we cannot say as much for the *subject-matter*. The subject-matter which deals with the four destructive winds and the sealing of the 144,000, is borrowed from Jewish sources.

vii. 1–3 from a Jewish source.

First, as to the four winds. The letting loose by the four angels of these destructive winds was, as the text implies, to take place after the sealing of the faithful was accomplished, or at all events shortly before the end. And yet these four angels are not again referred to directly in the Apocalypse. Hence we conclude, as many critics have already done, that our author has here used, as frequently, an older tradition. That such a tradition existed in various forms can be conclusively proved. I will quote two parallel situations to that in our text. In our text we are told that a *pause* in the judgments is commanded in order that during the pause the faithful may be

sealed. Similarly in 1 Enoch a like pause
takes place before the Deluge, for the preservation of Noah and his family. Thus in
lxvi. 1, 2 it is written : "And after that he
showed me the angels of punishment, who
are prepared to come and let loose all the
powers of the waters that are beneath in the
earth, in order to bring judgment and destruction on all who [abide and] dwell on the
earth. And the Lord of spirits gave com-
mandment to the angels who were going forth,
that they should not cause the waters to rise,
but should hold them in check ; for these angels
are over the powers of the waters." Now from
the opening verses of lxvii. we see that the
object of this pause is to give time for the
building of the ark—in other words, the pause
in judgment was ordered with a view to a preservation of the faithful in the ancient world,
just as here it is ordered with a view to the
sealing of the faithful at the end of the world.
Another remarkable parallel is to be found in
2 Bar. vi. 4 sqq. : "And I beheld, and, lo !
four angels standing at the four corners of the
city, each of them holding a torch of fire in
his hands. And another angel descended
from heaven, and said unto them : Hold your
torches, and do not light them till I tell you."
Here we have four angels ready to destroy

Jerusalem, and a fifth angel bidding them to pause, and not to destroy it till the sacred vessels were removed.

As regards the four destroying winds themselves, we can find traces of this conception from early in the second century B.C. to the second century A.D. Thus all the elements in vii. 1–3 can be explained from already existing tradition. Now, taking these facts into consideration together with the fact that the four winds in our text are not again referred to *directly*, we may reasonably conclude that our author has made use of an existing tradition to serve his purpose. Now, if we ask what this purpose was, the answer clearly is : the episode described in vii. 1–3 is introduced because a new order of plagues is about to ensue, and a pause must be made to secure the faithful against these plagues. In the verses that follow we learn that the faithful are secured by sealing them with the signet of God.

vii. 4–8 derived originally from a Jewish source.

We now pass to vii. 4–8. This section, which deals with the sealing of the 144,000, was not originally from the hand of our author, but was drawn by him from a Jewish or Jewish-

8

Christian source. If you ask on what ground this statement is based, the answer is : Since the tribes are definitely mentioned one by one, and the number sealed in each tribe is definitely fixed, the twelve tribes can only have meant the *literal* Israel in the original tradition. The Jewish origin of the tradition is further attested by the fact that the tribe of Dan is omitted. Dan was specially connected with the Antichrist in pre-Christian-Jewish tradition. But there is another point of interest in this list. Judah is put first, and not Levi. This is due to our author, or to a Christian recast of the passage. After the return from the captivity, Levi gradually acquired the first place. This we see clearly in the Testaments of the XII Patriarchs. Levi always takes precedence of Judah in this work, except in the Christian interpolations, where the order is not Levi, Judah, but Judah, Levi, because of our Lord's descent from Judah.

We conclude, therefore, that vii. 1–3 and vii. 4–8 go back to Jewish sources, but have been recast by our author and given a new significance.

Four irregularities in the list of the Twelve Tribes and their explanation.

But before we attempt to determine the new

significance attached to this section by our author, I must draw your attention to some irregularities in the list of the tribes. As you will see, if you consult the list, the tribes are mentioned in the following order :—Judah, Reuben, Gad, Asher, Naphtali, Manasseh, Simeon, Levi, Issachar, Zebulun, Joseph, Benjamin. In this list there are four irregularities. (*a*) Judah is placed first. (*b*) Dan is omitted. (*c*) Manasseh is given, though Manasseh is included already in Joseph, which follows. (*d*) The rest of the tribes are enumerated in an irregular order.

Judah is clearly mentioned first because from him is sprung the Messiah. This is a mark of Christian influence. (*d*) Before we discuss the difficulties in (*b*) and (*c*) we must examine that under (*d*), since if this can be solved the rest will be easier.

Now the present order of the tribes cannot be explained by any such irrelevancy as that of Grotius : "No order is observed, because all are equal in Christ." The text is unintelligible as it stands, and it is unintelligible because it is dislocated. This dislocation Dr. Buchanan Gray (*Encyc. Bib.* iv. 52 sq.) has recognised as due to an accidental transposition of vers. 7, 8, which originally stood before the last clause in vii. 5. By restoring these verses before the last clause of ver. 5, sanity is restored to the text, and the order of the Tribes becomes intelligible and illuminating. Thus the six sons of Leah, the first wife, come first—Judah, Reuben, Simeon, Levi, Issachar, Zebulun; next, the two sons of Rachel, the second wife, come second—Joseph and Benjamin; next, the two sons of Leah's handmaid — Gad and Asher; and, finally, we should have the two sons of Rachel's handmaid — Naphtali and Dan, but for certain reasons into which we shall now inquire we have Naphtali and Manasseh instead.

We have now to discover why Dan was omitted from this list and Manasseh inserted in his stead. Manasseh is obviously *de trop* here, since Manasseh is included in the tribe of Joseph; and Joseph is undoubtedly original, since the list obviously aims at giving the sons of Rachel, as it has given the sons of Leah, and not two of Rachel's sons and one grandson, as it does in its present form. Manifestly grandsons have no *locus standi* in this list. Here Manasseh has been substituted for Dan—the missing son of Rachel's handmaid. This substitution has made the list illogical. We have therefore to inquire, (b) Why was Dan omitted, and by whom?

Many explanations have been offered by modern scholars, but the true explanation as well as the most ancient is that propounded by Irenæus. According to Irenæus, Dan was omitted because the Antichrist was to spring from Dan. The same statement appears in Hippolytus, and later in Andreas. That this tradition is pre-Christian and Jewish, I have shown in the notes to the Test. of Dan v. 6, 7, in my edition of the Testaments of the XII Patriarchs. Further, in a work on *The Antichrist Legend*, 171 sq., Bousset has proved at length that this interpretation of our text was that which was generally accepted in the Early Christian Church; for in addition to Irenæus and Hippolytus, it was supported by Eucharius, Augustine, Jacob of Edessa, Theodoret, Arethas, Bede. This interpretation is accepted by Holtzmann, Johannes Weiss, Selwyn, Moffatt and others.

(*c*) Now that we have seen why and by whom Dan was omitted, it becomes easier to explain the inclusion of Manasseh among the twelve sons of Jacob. The gap in the twelve, caused by the omission of Dan, had to be filled up somehow, although it could not be logically. The original Jewish author of the section therefore fell back on the grandsons of Jacob, and the only grandsons of Jacob that gave a name to a tribe were Ephraim and Manasseh. He adopted Manasseh in preference to Ephraim—

possibly on the ground that Ephraim was frequently used in the prophets to designate the ten tribes of northern Israel from the time of Isaiah onwards. It is so used in Sirach. The irregularities of this list are thus, I think, satisfactorily explained—the placing of Judah first, the omission of Dan, the inclusion of Manasseh, and, finally, the unintelligible order of the rest, as owing to an accidental transposition of the text.

Having now recognised the extraordinary irregularities in the list of the Twelve Tribes, as well as the fact that vii. 1–3 and viii. 4–8 go back to Jewish sources, we have now to determine the new significance which these two sections have acquired by being recast and incorporated in a Christian work.

What is the meaning of the Sealing?

What, then, is the new significance that our author gives to the sealing of the 144,000? This is really one of the most important questions in the Apocalypse, if we are to understand it aright.

Danger of being misled by Old Testament parallels.

Nearly every commentator has given one and the same interpretation to this passage. The

general accord of scholars in this interpretation is due to the influence of Old Testament
parallels.   Now the Old Testament is a good
guide in the interpretation of the New Testament, but its guidance can be accepted safely
only with limitations.   Let me give one of the
many instances that might be cited, wherein
the same phrase occurs in the Old Testament
and in the New Testament, and yet has assumed
quite a new meaning in the latter.   The Book
of Life in the Old Testament, which is referred to
in Exod. xxxii. 32, where Moses prays on behalf
of sinful Israel : " If thou wilt not forgive them
their sin, blot me, I pray thee, out of the book
which thou hast written."   This book is again
referred to in Ps. lxix. 28.   It was the register
of the citizens of the theocratic community.
To have one's name written in the Book of Life
in the Old Testament, implied the privilege of
participating in the temporal blessings of the
Theocracy, as in Isa. iv. 3, Ezek. xiii. 9 ; while
to be blotted out of this Book, Exod. xxxii. 32,
Ps. lxix. 28, meant exclusion from these blessings.   Now in the Old Testament, that is,
in the Prophets, the Law, and the Wisdom
literature, this expression was absolutely limited
to this world ; but in Dan. xii. 1 it is transformed through the influence of the new conception of the Kingdom, and distinctly refers

to citizenship in a spiritual Kingdom, to an immortality of blessedness.

This single example will show how carefully we are to guard against assuming that the same words or phrases, in the Old Testament and New Testament, must necessarily have the same meaning.   On the contrary, we may assume that all Old Testament conceptions which were capable of spiritual development have changed their meaning more or less, either in the course of the two centuries preceding the Christian era, or especially by their adoption into the sphere of Christian thought.

Now let us return to the question immediately before us.

According to all interpreters, except Düster-dieck, up to the present day, the object of the sealing was to secure against physical evil, as in the Old Testament and Judaism.

What is the meaning of the sealing of the faithful in its present context ?   The practically universal reply of commentators is that (*a*) it means *preservation from physical evil.*   Now I quite concede that in this tradition *in its Jewish form* this was the meaning, and in this connection appeal is rightly made to Exod. xii. 7, 13, 22, where all those who had sprinkled the posts and lintels of their houses were to be saved from the destroying angel. The same meaning attaches to Ezek. ix. 3–11, where the six destroying angels are to destroy old man, young man, and maiden, little children and women—in fact, every one who had not the mark of God on his forehead. This Judaistic conception of *preservation from physical evil* is present also in the little Jewish Apocalypse in the Gospels—Mark xiii. 17–20, and the parallels in Matthew and Luke. That it was a current Jewish expectation we see in part from this interpolated Jewish Apocalypse. But if any one were disposed to cavil at this evidence, we can refer him to irrefragable proof in the Psalms of Solomon xv. 8–10, which were written about the middle of the first century B.C. From this Psalm we learn that "the sign of the Lord is to be upon the righteous for their salvation" (τὸ σημεῖον τοῦ θεοῦ ἐπὶ δικαίους εἰς σωτηρίαν), and the nature of this salvation is defined by the words that follow: for "famine and the sword and pestilence were to be far from the righteous" (λιμὸς καὶ ῥομφαία καὶ θάνατος μακρὰν ἀπὸ δικαίων).

Now I ask your close attention here, and pray you to observe the contrast between the expectation in our text and in this Psalm. In the Psalm the sign is placed on the brows of

the righteous to secure them from the eschatological woes that follow, namely, "famine,
sword, and pestilence"; whereas in our text the
sign is not placed on the brows of the faithful
till after these very woes had taken place ; for
in vi. 8, after the opening of the fourth Seal, it
is said : "There was given unto them authority
to kill with the sword, and with famine, and
with pestilence." The likeness of our context
to, and yet its essential divergence from, this
Psalm, appears further in xv. 6, 7, where the
righteous are promised immunity from all the
evils that are to be sent against the wicked
in the last days. Furthermore, according to
this Psalmist "the mark of destruction was
to be set on the foreheads of the sinners"
(τὸ γὰρ σημεῖον τῆς ἀπωλείας ἐπὶ τοῦ μετώπου
αὐτῶν), and that accordingly "famine and the
sword and pestilence would pursue and over-
take the sinners," who would "perish in
the day of the judgment of the Lord for
ever."

If preservation from physical evil had been
intended by our author, the sealing must have
taken place before the first Seal, and not in
the midst of the cosmic catastrophes of the
sixth. Vitringa feels this so strongly, that he
maintains that vii. 1–8 should be read before
vi. 12–17 ; whilst Hengstenberg would place

this section before chap. vi. Holtzmann in the last edition says that the difficulty involved in the position of the sealing after the sixth Seal has never been explained.

Düsterdieck's view that it is secured against spiritual apostasy.

(*b*) At last the consciousness of the wrongness of the accepted interpretation came home to Düsterdieck and led him to propound the view that *it is not from physical evil, but from spiritual apostasy*, under the last and greatest trials that should befall the world, *that the sealing is designed to secure the faithful*. Now I confess that for a time I accepted this view. It belongs decidedly to a higher plane than the generally accepted interpretation : the securing against spiritual apostasy is unquestionably a nobler object for the sealing than preservation from physical evil. But, after I had written a considerable section of my Commentary, it came home to me in turn that Düsterdieck's interpretation would not meet the difficulty, and that the immediate object of the sealing was to be discovered in ix. 4, where the implication of the text is, that it is from demonic agencies that the sealed are to be secured, and not from physical evil in any form. This verse runs :

"And it was said unto them that they should not hurt the grass of the earth, neither any green thing, neither any tree; but only such men as have not the seal of God on their foreheads."

This verse (ix. 4) suggests the right interpretation of the passage, which is as follows:

The true secret of the sealing was to secure against demonic agencies.

(*c*) In our text, therefore, the sealing of the faithful was designed to secure them from demonic agencies in the coming reign of the Antichrist. As this reign, so full of superhuman horrors, was about to begin, the sealing was carried out just then, and not earlier and not later. This sealing did not secure against social or cosmic evils, such as had already occurred and would again occur; nor did it secure against martyrdom, as we learn in xviii. 24: "And in her was found the blood of prophets, and of saints, and of all that have been slain upon the earth," but only against diabolic or demonic powers, as we see in ix. 4. The sealing provides the spiritual help that the faithful needed against the coming manifestation of Satanic wickedness linked with seemingly supreme power. With this help the weakest servant of God needed not to dread the mightiest of his spiritual foes. The seal of God engraved on his brow marked him as God's property, and as such assured him of God's protection. But it did not in itself secure him against spiritual apostasy. Against this Christ warns the elect in Matt. xxiv. 24, and requires of them unfailing endurance (Mark xiii. 13, "he that endureth to the end, the same shall be saved"). If the elect bear with patience the natural trials incident to their faithful discipleship of Christ, then He on His part will preserve them from the superhuman trials that are about to come on the whole world, as He promises to the Seer in iii. 10 : "Because thou hast kept the word of my patience, I also will keep thee from the hour of trial, that hour which is to come upon the whole world, to try them that dwell upon the earth."

The reasonableness of this view appears clearly from another standpoint. In the Old Testament, with its belief in a heathen school, the righteous could enjoy the divine protection only on this earth, if they were to enjoy it at all ; and hence a long and happy life, fenced from physical ill, was the natural prerogative of the faithful. But in later times, and above all in the New Testament where the doctrine of a future life was fully and finally established, the centre of interest passed from things material to things spiritual. Protection—not from physical ill and death, but from the demonic or Satanic enemies of the spirit—became the supreme aim of the faithful.

The meaning attached to the sealing was early transferred to Christian baptism.

The above interpretation has been lost to Christendom for 1600 years or thereabouts; but in the first three centuries we can find traces of its existence, and recognise the reason why the true interpretation of the sealing of the 144,000 was lost to the knowledge of the Church. The ideas, originally associated with the sealing in our text, passed over at a very early date to Christian baptism. How early this was we shall not attempt to determine here. In any case the ideas of the sealing in our text and baptism were associated in the second century A.D., and the way for this association was made easy by the fact that the term "seal," σφραγίς, was used of baptism. To baptism, of course, there is no allusion in our text; but baptism, according to early Christian beliefs, combined the two ideas here present : (1) it marked the baptized as God's (or Christ's) property ; (2) it secured the baptized against demonic powers. Let me quote some passages from writings of the

second, third, and fourth centuries bearing
on these points. In the Acts of Thomas
xxvi. we read: "Give unto us the seal:
for we have heard you say that God . . .
recognises His own sheep by His own seal."
Here baptism is the seal: it is also the
outward mark distinguishing the believer from
the unbeliever. Again, in the same work
(p. 68, ed. Bonnet) baptism is clearly designated as a seal. "Give me the seal in Christ,
and let me receive the laver of immortality."
Other passages designating baptism as a
seal are to be found in *2 Clement*, *The Acts
of Paul*, and the *Martyrdom of Paul*.
But from these passages which designate
baptism as a seal of God, we shall now proceed
to those which combine with the ideas of the
sealing in baptism those of recognition and
defence. In Clement of Alex., *Selections from
the Prophets*, xii., we find : "When these things
are fulfilled, then the seal follows, in order
that what is holy may be preserved to God";
and in *Summaries from Theodotus*, "Sealed
by the Father, the Son, and the Holy Spirit,
he is not open to the attacks of any power";
in Cyril, *Catechetical Lectures*, i. 3 (fourth
century), "There He bestows the wondrous
seal of salvation, which demons tremble at
and angels recognise, so that the former are

driven to flight and the latter cherish it as
their own." At the beginning of this century
we find that in Lactantius the entire meaning
attached to sealing in our text is conveyed
to baptism. Thus in the *Divine Institutions*,
iv. 26, he speaks of "Christ being slain for
the salvation of all who have written on
their foreheads the sign of the blood—that is,
the sign of the Cross"; and again (iv. 27),
"the presence of Christians bearing this sign,
when attending on their masters at the
heathen sacrifice, puts to flight the gods of
their masters, *i.e.* "the demons": and "since
the demons can neither approach those on
whom they have seen the heavenly mark,
nor injure those whom the immortal sign as an
impregnable wall protects, they harass them
by men, and persecute them by the hands of
others." Here the sign of the cross discharges
the very same function as the seal affixed to
the foreheads of the faithful in our text.

I have now shown that in the writings of
the second, third, and fourth centuries are
found survivals of the original and true interpretation of the sealing of the faithful in
our text, though in these writings the significance of the sealing has already been
transferred to baptism,—a transference that
was made easy by the fact that from very

early Christian times baptism itself was described as "a sealing."

Demonic dangers expected by Judaism in the last days.

I think I have now proved, first, that the context itself requires the interpretation I have advanced, and secondly, that traces of this interpretation appear in the early centuries in connection with baptism. But the lines of evidence are not yet exhausted. I will now, in the third place, show that such demonic dangers were expected by Judaism in the last days. Thus in the Testament of Dan vi. 1–3, an inroad of demonic beings and a special strengthening of Israel against them by Michael is predicted ; and in the first century A.D. we read in 2 Bar. xxvii. 9, that the final tribulation is to be marked by a multitude of portents and incursions of demons.

I have now given sufficient evidence in regard to what in my opinion is the only tenable interpretation of the sealing of the 144,000. Let me now resume the main points I have dealt with, and give this interpretation in its original meaning, and its true bearing for after times.

9

The original and permanent significance of the sealing.

The sealing is to secure the servants of God against the attacks of demonic powers coming into manifestation; for the powers of Satan are about to make their last struggle for the mastery of the world.   In the past their attacks on man had been restricted to attacks on man's spiritual being, and had therefore been hidden, invisible, and mysterious; but now at the end of time they are to come forth from their mysterious background, and make open battle with God and His hosts for the possession of the earth and of mankind.   The hidden mystery of wickedness, the secret source of all the haunting horrors and crimes and failures and sins of the past, was about to reveal itself—the Antichrist was to become incarnate and appear armed with all but almighty power.   With such foes the faithful felt themselves wholly unfit to do battle. With the rage and hostility of man, with an invisible Satan and his invisible hosts, they could cope, but with their ghostly enemy and his myrmidons about to manifest themselves openly on earth they dared not engage. And so, just on the eve of this epiphany of Satan, God seals His servants on their foreheads to show that they are His own possession, and that no embodied or disembodied spirit of the wicked one can do them hurt. So much for the contemporary and original meaning of this passage. Now as to its deepest and permanent significance, the sealing means the outward manifestation of character. The hidden goodness of God's servants is at last blazoned outwardly, and the divine name that was written in secret day by day and year by year by God's Spirit on their hearts, is now engraved openly on their brows by the very signet-ring of the Living God. In the reign of Antichrist—in the last times, whether in this world or in some far distant one, goodness and evil, righteousness and sin, must come into their fullest manifestation and antagonism. Character must ultimately enter on the stage of finality. In this sense, too, we must interpret the words of St. Paul in Rom. viii. 19: "For the earnest longing of the creation waiteth for the manifestation of the sons of God."

Having now dealt with the meaning of the sealing of the 144,000, we have next to ask who these 144,000 are, and likewise who are the great multitude out of every nation and tribe and people and tongue standing before God and the Lamb, arrayed in white robes, and with palms in their hands. The answer

to this question is, in short, as follows. Chap.
vii. refers not to all Christians, but only to the
generation of believers contemporary with the
author, first as militant on earth, vii. 1–8, and
next as triumphant in heaven, vii. 9–17.

vii. 1–8 refers only to the generation contemporary with the Apocalyptist.

Now, first of all, it is clear that vii. 1–8 deals
only with the generation of the faithful contemporary with the author; for *in the thought
of the Seer it is only this generation* that has
to endure the last and greatest tribulation.
To preserve it against the superhuman evils
about to burst upon the world, the progress of
the plagues is stayed, and the faithful are
secured against such as are of a demonic
character, being sealed as God's own possession.

vii. 9–17 refers to the Apocalyptist's own generation.

It is no less clear that the great host in
vii. 9–17 does not embrace the whole Church,
but only those who had come out of the great
tribulation. Not only on account of the
definite article and the distinctive epithet
μεγάλης, "great," but also on account of the
whole vision and its relation to the rest of the
book, it is wholly inadmissible to treat the

great tribulation quite generally as any and every tribulation that is incident to the life of faithful discipleship. The scribe of the Codex Alexandrinus was apparently conscious of this difficulty, and accordingly omitted the two articles and read " from great tribulation "; but all the other MSS are against this reading. It is the last and greatest tribulation that, according to our author, is to befall his own generation ; and vii. 9–17 deals only with the great multitude which had gone, were going, or were to go through it faithfully.

The two classes, therefore, described in this chapter belong to the generation contemporary with the Apocalyptist. Of whom are they respectively composed, the 144,000 and the great multitude ?

Those sealed in vii. 4–8 are the spiritual Israel of the Apocalyptist's own time.

Now as regards the 144,000, we shall find that in their present context they are not Christians belonging to Israel after the flesh, but to the spiritual Israel. In the original tradition we found that these 144,000 were Jews or Jewish-Christians. It is true that several able scholars, such as Düsterdieck, Holtzmann, Bousset and others, have maintained that in their present context they are

Jewish-Christians, and that they are in no case to be identified with the countless host in vii. 9–17; for in the one case we have a definite number, in the other an indefinite one; in the one a definite body of Jewish-Christians, in the other a multitude of all nations and peoples; in the one, the last great woe is surmounted and left behind, in the other it is still impending. Now the last objection is of no weight. The vision in vii. 9–17 is proleptic, anticipatory. It prophesies the outcome of the present life. The two visions presuppose different conditions—the one a phase of the Church militant, the other a phase of the Church triumphant. From this standpoint no objection can be maintained against the identity of the two groups under different conditions of time and place.

And other objections, when considered in the light of the thought which underlies the sealing of the faithful, lose forthwith any force they seemed to have. For since we have seen from iii. 10 that the great tribulation was about to come upon *the whole world*, and from vii. 4–8 that the essential danger connected with this tribulation was its demonic character, and that the sole object of the sealing was to preserve the faithful against demonic powers, it follows inevitably that the sealing must be co-extensive with the peril, and must, therefore, embrace the entire Christian community— alike Jewish and Gentile. For the necessary grace of preservation from demonic influences cannot be accorded to the faithful descended from Israel according to the flesh, and withheld from the faithful descended from Israel according to the spirit, in a work of so universalistic import as the Apocalypse. In other words, the 144,000 belong not to the literal, but to the spiritual Israel, and are composed of all nations and peoples and languages.

From this standpoint the number 144,000 presents no difficulty. It is merely a symbolical and not a definite number. The real explanation of its appearance here is, that it is part of a tradition, taken over by our author, and a part to which he attaches no definite significance in its new context. The part of the tradition with which he is concerned is the sealing. This element is of overwhelming significance. It is the measure adopted by God to secure His servants against the manifestation and, for the time, victorious self-assertion of the Satanic world. The other elements of the tradition,—although taken into the text, *are of the slightest concern, or of none at all to our author*. This is frequently his practice. We have already

seen it in vii. 1–3, where the main idea is the
pause, which is commanded in the succession
of the plagues, in order to effect this sealing.
As regards the four winds,—another element
in the tradition,—our author does not refer to
them again directly.

From what precedes, therefore, we conclude
that the 144,000 belong to the spiritual Israel
—in other words, to the Christian Church
throughout the world, composed of Jew and
Gentile; and, in the next place, that they
represent only the present generation of
believers.

The great multitude in vii. 9–17 are identical with the 144,000.

We have now to deal more fully with vii.
9–17. This section is not the work of a redactor, nor is it borrowed from an earlier and
alien source; for every word, verse, and nearly
every phrase is related in point of *diction and
meaning* to the rest of the Apocalypse. Into
a detailed proof of this statement I cannot
enter here, but I think you may safely take it
that this section is the work of our author.

Next, "the great multitude" in this section
is identical with the 144,000 in vii. 4–8. We
have already shown that "the great multitude"
embraces not the Christians and the faithful

of all time, but only the Christian contemporaries of the Seer—the faithful of the
present generation. Since the 144,000 refer
to the same body, it is clear that "the great
multitude" and the 144,000 are identical
qualitatively and quantitatively.

vii. 9–17 was originally a description of all the blessed after the final judgment.

But this does not appear to have been the
meaning of this vision in its original form.
On good grounds we conclude that the vision
was our author's own, but that originally it
had another application. The great multitude
represented the entire body of the blessed in
heaven, after the final judgment. But it does
not do so in its present context, but represents
the martyrs of the last days serving God in
heaven before the final judgment. I shall now
attempt to prove this statement. vii. 9–17
seems to have been a parallel in its original form
to xxi. 1–8, and like it to have represented the
entire body of the blessed after the final judgment. For, in the first place, the same phraseology is used of the blessed. Thus, whereas it
is said that He that sitteth on the throne shall
dwell over them, vii. 15, so in xxi. 3 it is
written that the tabernacle of God shall be
with men, and He shall dwell with them

σκηνώσει in both cases); in vii. 17 it is said
that God will "wipe away every tear from
their eyes": the same statement reappears in
xxi. 5; while in vii. 16 it is said that "they
shall hunger no more, neither thirst any more;
neither shall the sun strike upon them, nor any
heat"; in xxi. 4, we read "neither shall there be
mourning, nor crying, nor pain any more."

Secondly, there is no phrase in this section
which in itself definitely limits the description
to the martyrs. The phrases that demand such
a limitation are, as we shall see, of an indirect
though cogent character, and are due to our
author's adaptation of an independent vision to
a new context. Thirdly, the clause "which no
man could number" can hardly have been
written originally of a section of the righteous
(*i.e.* the martyrs), but fittingly describes the
countless hosts of all the blessed. Fourthly, if
we disregard the phrases "the great tribulation"
and "in the temple," the whole impression of
the vision is that it deals with a final condition
of the blessed in heaven, in which they render
perfect and ceaseless service to God, and all the
sorrow and pain of the earthly life are in the
past, vii. 17.

Lastly, after the final judgment all the
faithful were to be clothed in white.

On these grounds this section appears origin-

ally to have been a description of all the
blessed after the final judgment; and so most
scholars take this to be its meaning in its
present context.

*But in its present context vii. 9–17 refers to
the martyrs of the great tribulation.*

But, as we have already seen, this cannot be
its meaning. The great multitude embraces
not all the faithful, but only the faithful that
issued victoriously from " the great tribulation."
Next, if we take οἱ ἐρχόμενοι as an imperfect
participle = " those who are coming " (not " those
who have come "),[1] the great tribulation is still
in progress, the end of the world is not yet
come, the final judgment is yet to be held, and
all who belong to the great multitude are
martyrs; for all are already clothed in white
(vi. 9). Thirdly, if we may use xxi. 22 (" I
saw no temple therein ") as an exponent of our
author's views, we may infer that there will be
no temple in the new heaven and new earth after
the final judgment. Fourthly, in xxi. 4 the
words " there shall be no more death " postulate
a time after the final judgment. It is note-
worthy that no such expression occurs in the

---

[1] If the text here is translated from the Hebrew, then it
would = הבאים. This Hebrew phrase could = " those that have
come," " those that are coming," or " those about to come."

present section. Fifthly, our interpretation
receives support from the general theme of the
book—the glorification of martyrdom, and
especially from the place of this section in
the book; for the time which it deals with
forms the very eve of the last and greatest
tribulation.

Hence we conclude that the vision in its
present form refers to the martyrs of the great
tribulation, though it exhibits survivals of ideas
and statements which appear to show that
originally it bore a very different meaning.

Now, before I leave this passage, I must refer
to a very important question which arises in
this chapter, and which, if rightly understood,
has a great weight in reference to the problems
already discussed.

*The white garments are the spiritual bodies
which the martyrs receive before the final
judgment.*

This question is—What is the meaning of
"the white garments" in which the blessed are
clothed?

On a full discussion of the meaning of these
garments, I cannot enter here. These garments
have already been referred to in iii. 5 and vi.
11. In the former, they are promised to the
living Christians as a gift hereafter to be

received; in the latter, they are described as already given. Now, in the last passage the recipients of the white garments are the martyrs under the altar. The martyrs, moreover, receive these garments before the final judgment. All I can say now is, that these garments are the spiritual bodies which the faithful are to receive. According to our Apocalypse, only the martyrs receive their spiritual bodies before the judgment, just as it is only they who share in the first resurrection in order to enjoy the 1000 years' reign with Christ. That the white garments have this meaning I hope to prove elsewhere.

CHAPTER V.

SUMMARY OF CONCLUSIONS ALREADY ARRIVED AT IN CHAPTER VII.

BEFORE I enter on the interpretation of chaps. viii.–ix. it will be helpful to resume a few of the conclusions at which we have already arrived. Chap. vi., which we have not discussed, but the general meaning of which is obvious, deals with the opening of the first six seals. After the opening of each seal some woe or calamity followed, of a social or cosmic character; and whatever view we take as to the date of the events of the sixth Seal, there can be no question as to the fact that the first five seals refer to the past and immediate present. Passing now from chap. vi. to chap. vii., we found that a pause in the judgment is enjoined, and we learnt from the context itself as well as from the analogous passages in Apocalyptic literature, that this pause was commanded, in order that during it the faithful might be sealed, to secure them against woes or judgments of a new type that were impending.

Now the fact that this sealing had not taken place at an earlier period at once struck us as surprising. This fact made it clear that the object of the sealing was not to secure the faithful against physical evils, else it would have taken place not at the close of the sixth Seal, but before the first. The coming woes are, therefore, to be of a character quite distinct from those already past, since special measures have to be taken to secure the faithful against them. They were, as ix. 4 clearly shows, to be of a demonic character. The reign of Antichrist, with all its superhuman horrors, was about to begin, and so the sealing was carried out just then, and not earlier, and not later. This sealing did not secure against physical or social or cosmic evils, such as had already occurred, and would again occur; least of all did it secure against martyrdom : but it secured the faithful against the coming outward manifestation of demonic power, the epiphany of Satan and his kingdom. With this help the weakest servant of God need not dread the mightiest of his spiritual foes. The seal of God, engraven on his brow, marked him off as God's own property, and as such assured him of God's protection. The powers of Satan were about to make their last struggle for the mastery of the world. In the past their efforts had been hidden, invisible, mysterious, but now, at the end of time, they are to issue forth from their mysterious background and make open battle with God and His hosts for the possession of earth and heaven.[1] The hidden mystery of wickedness was about to reveal itself, the Antichrist was in some sense to become incarnate, and appear armed with all but almighty power. Against such spiritual foes coming into manifestation, the faithful needed special help, and this was accorded to them, and that just on the eve of the epiphany of the Antichrist and Satan. Behind this vivid symbolism we found truths of deep and permanent significance. The sealing means the outward manifestation of character. The hidden goodness of God's servants is at last blazoned

[1] To the prophet of old as to the Apocalyptist the end—the culmination of evil and the final triumph of righteousness—was always in the immediate future. For ourselves, it is of small concern whether this end comes during the existence of our planet or many millenniums after its extinction. But it is an essential article of every true man's creed, that some day in the far off æons evil will be absolutely annihilated throughout the universe, and truth and love and purity will ultimately prevail for evermore. "Of that day and hour knoweth no man, not even the angels of heaven, nor yet the Son, but the Father only" (Matt. xxiv. 36). Moreover, in this cosmic strife all true men who, in the present and in the countless ages of the past, have already fought the good fight, will, with all the faithful of the coming ages, maintain with ever growing power this truceless warfare, till at last evil is swept over the bank of annihilation, and the universe is won for Christ and God.

outwardly, and the divine name, which has
been written secretly by God's Spirit on their
hearts, is now engraven openly on their brows
by the very signet-ring of the Living God.
In the last times, goodness and evil, righteousness and sin, come into the fullest manifestation
and antagonism.   Character must ultimately
enter on the stage of finality.

We arrived at other important conclusions
in our study of chap. vii., but with these we are
not here immediately concerned.   But if we
would understand chaps. viii. and ix., we must
not lose sight of the right meaning of the
sealing in chap. vii.

Chapter viii. and its meaning.

Let us now study chap. viii.   It begins with
the opening of the seventh Seal, and the
strange silence that ensued in heaven for the
space of half an hour.

Into the significance of this silence in connection with the first five verses we are not
yet in a position to penetrate.   We must first
pass on to section viii. 7–12, which deals with
the first four trumpets.   For the nature of the
fresh plagues or woes we have already been
prepared in vii. 4–8, where the faithful were
sealed, in order to secure them from the
coming demonic or Satanic attacks.   After

10

this sealing the expectation is natural and inevitable that the next plagues to befall the inhabiters of the earth should be demonic.

Following on vii. 4–8, the four Trumpets, viii. 7–12, appear foreign to the text.

But, as the text stands, so far is this from being the case that we find a fresh series of colourless cosmic visitations following on the first four Trumpets, viii. 7–12, whereas the demonic plagues do not begin till the fifth Trumpet. Thus the first four Trumpets not only arrest the natural development of the book, but they also introduce an alien element at this stage. Something must be wrong here, and we are thus *a priori* disposed to doubt the originality of the first four Trumpets.

Critical grounds for the rejection of viii. 7–12 as an interpolation.

And when we come to examine these four Trumpets our doubts are transformed into convictions, and we discover that whereas the heptadic structure of the Seals and the Bowls is fundamental and original, the heptadic structure of the Trumpets is secondary and superinduced.

Let us read the description of the first four Trumpets in viii. 7–12.

7 " And the first sounded, and there followed

hail and fire mingled with blood, and they were cast upon the earth : and the third part of the earth was burnt up, and the third part of the trees was burnt up, and all green grass was burnt up.

8 And the second angel sounded, and as it were a great mountain burning with fire was cast into the sea : and the third part of the sea became blood ; 9 And there died the third part of the creatures which were in the sea, even they that had life ; and the third part of the ships were destroyed.

10 And the third angel sounded, and there fell from heaven a great star, burning as a torch, and it fell upon the third part of the rivers, and upon the fountains of the waters ; 11 And the name of the star is called Wormwood, and the third part of the waters became wormwood ; and many men died of the waters, because they were made bitter.

12 And the fourth angel sounded, and the third part of the sun was smitten, and the third part of the moon, and the third part of the stars ; that the third part of them should be darkened, and the day should not shine for the third part of it and the night in like manner."

The heptadic structure, as we have already said, is secondary in the case of the Trumpets.

For (1) the first four Trumpets are conventional and monotonous. One-third of the chief things mentioned is destroyed in each, except in viii. 11, where, instead of the third of mankind—τὸ τρίτον τῶν ἀνθρώπων, which was clearly the original text—we have the strange phrase πολλοὶ τῶν ἀνθρώπων,[1] where, according to our author's style, we should expect simply πολλοὶ ἄνθρωποι, or rather ἄνθρωποι πολλοί, since in the Apocalypse πολύς is always postpositive. But the reason for this change is not obscure. Since the invasion of the earth by the "twice ten thousand times ten thousand" demonic horsemen results in the destruction of one-third of mankind, ix. 18 (sixth Trumpet—second Woe), the same result cannot here be fittingly ascribed to the third Trumpet. Hence the original phrase "one-third of mankind" is here changed into "many men." (2) The first Trumpet conflicts with the sixth. For after the first Trumpet we read that "all green grass was burnt up" (πᾶς χόρτος χλωρὸς κατεκάη), and yet after the sixth Trumpet

[1] I cannot find this strange phrase elsewhere. The nearest parallel is Luke i. 16, πολλοὺς τῶν υἱῶν Ἰσραήλ. But here the genitive denotes a definite number: cf. Matt. iii. 7; Acts iv. 4, viii. 7, xiii. 43, xviii. 8, xix. 18, xxvi. 10. In the Fourth Gospel, πολλοὶ τῶν does not, as Abbott (*Johannine Grammar*,

is sounded it is presupposed to be uninjured;
for the demonic locusts in ix. 4 are bidden not
to "hurt the grass of the earth." (3) The first
four Trumpets are described as plain objective
events, but the visionary nature of the fifth
and sixth Trumpets is clearly marked. Cf.
ix. 1, "The fifth angel sounded, and I saw";
ix. 13, "the sixth angel sounded, and I heard."
The seventh Trumpet is also of a visionary
character (cf. xi. 19, xii. 1). (4) When compared with the Seals that precede and the
Bowls that follow, the first four Trumpets are
colourless and weak repetitions. Thus contrast
the darkening of one-third of the stars, and
the falling of two of them after the second,
third, and fourth Trumpets, viii. 8, 10, 12,
with the falling of all the stars to the earth,
as unripe figs when shaken by the wind, after
the sixth Seal, vi. 13; the darkening of one-
third of the sun, viii. 12 (in the fourth Trumpet), with the intensification of his fires (so as
"to scorch men with fire") after the fourth
Bowl, xvi. 8 sq. ; the change of one-third of the
sea into blood, and the embittering of one-third
of the rivers after the second and third Trump-

p. 89) points out, occur, but only a modified form of it with a
verb or participle interposed. The nearest parallels to the
phrase πολλοὶ τῶν ἀνθρώπων are to be found in the LXX
(1 Esd. viii. 17; 2 Macc. iv. 35, 42, vi. 24 (πολλοὶ τῶν νέων);
3 Macc. ii. 26.

pets, viii. 8–11, with the turning of the entire
sea and rivers and springs into blood, and the
destruction of every living thing in the sea,
after the second and third bowls, xvi. 3–7.
(5) The first four Trumpets exhibit a somewhat
different diction and style. But the linguistic
argument is not as decisive as elsewhere.
There are two irregularities which belong to
our author : the first—ὡς ὄρος μέγα = " the
likeness of a great mountain "—belongs indeed
to our author's style, but it is also a typical
apocalyptic idiom, and is found elsewhere in
1 Enoch and the LXX ; the second, however,
is more characteristic of our author, *i.e.* the
syntactical irregularity, τῶν κτισμάτων . . . τὰ
ἔχοντα ψυχάς.

On the other hand, we find in viii. 8, πυρὶ
καιόμενον ; but elsewhere πυρί or a like noun
follows this verb. Cf. xix. 20, xxi. 8. In viii. 7
we have μεμιγμένα ἐν, but in xv. 2 the ἐν is omitted.
In viii. 12 we find σκοτίζειν, but in ix. 2 (cf.
xvi. 10) σκοτοῦν is the verb used by our author.
Finally, in viii. 1, 3–5, 13, the order is purely
Semitic, the verb in all cases beginning the
sentence except in viii. 3, where the subject
precedes the verb. And yet even here the
subject in Hebrew would rightly precede the
verb, since it is emphatic. In viii. 7–12, on
the other hand, the subject precedes the verb

thrice in viii. 7, twice in viii. 8, once in viii. 9, and once in viii. 10, twice in viii. 11, twice in viii. 12—that is, in all eleven times.

We have now found that viii. 7–12 is open to critical objections of every kind. The nature of the Sealing is wholly against it, which leads us to expect, not a conventional and colourless repetition of the physical plagues which occur elsewhere in the book, but plagues of a demonic character. And, further, from an examination of viii. 7–12 itself, we have found that the internal evidence is strongly against its authenticity. And, finally, we have recognised that, instead of carrying forward the development of the thought and action, these verses distinctly interfere with it, and take us back again to where we were at the beginning of chap. vi.

Accordingly, we cannot but regard them as inserted by a later editor of the book, who failed to apprehend the meaning of the Sealing, and the movement of the author's thought.

Changes in the text introduced by the inter-polator of viii. 7–12.

Now that we have discovered the secondary character of viii. 7–12, we have next to study the changes made in the text by this interpolator in order to prepare the way for his interpolation.

First of all, viii. 2 is an intrusion. This verse reads, "And I saw the seven angels, which stand before God ; and there were given unto them seven trumpets." You will observe, as J. Weiss has pointed out, that in this verse the mention of the seven angels, to whom the seven trumpets were given, comes as an interruption between the opening of the seventh Seal and the offering of the prayers of the saints, and yet the angels do not take any part in the action till viii. 6. This, it is true, would not in itself constitute a valid objection against the originality of viii. 2, and in its present position, but there are other and stronger objections not hitherto observed.

Grounds for regarding viii. 2 as an intrusion in its present position and in its present form.

For (1), viii. 2 in its present position is against the structure of the book, in analogous situations elsewhere. Thus it is to be noted that the *introduction* to the seventh trumpet (*i.e.* the third Woe), xi. 14, 15, is closed by thunderings and lightnings in xi. 19 ; and the introduction to the seventh Bowl, xvi. 17, by a series of like phenomena, xvi. 18 ; and that between the sounding of the seventh Trumpet and the thunderings, and the pouring forth of the seventh Bowl and the thunderings and

lightnings, there is no intrusive reference to any
further fresh visitation.   In like manner, we
infer that between the opening of the seventh
Seal and the outburst of thunderings and lightnings which follow in viii. 5, there was originally
no intrusive reference to any fresh visitation,
such as those of the Trumpets or Woes, as in
viii. 2.   (2) Again, viii. 2 not only comes as an
interruption and conflicts with the structure of
the book in analogous passages elsewhere, but
it has also by its intrusion here debarred the
recognition of the true meaning of the Solemn
Silence for half an hour in heaven, viii. 1.
The praises and thanksgivings of all the
mighty hierarchies of heaven are hushed, in
order that the prayers of the suffering saints
on earth may be heard before the throne of
God.   When this interpolated verse is removed,
the connection between ver. 1 and ver. 3—
between the silence in heaven in ver. 1 and
the presentation of the prayers of the faithful
on the golden altar before God in vers. 3–5—
at once springs to light.   The praises and
thanksgivings of the heavenly hosts are hushed,
in order that the prayers of the suffering saints
on earth may be heard before the throne of
God.

The recovery of the meaning of the text is
thus due to a critical examination of the text.

It was not until I had discovered that viii. 7–12
was an intrusion, and consequently viii. 2, that
the true interpretation of the solemn silence in
heaven burst upon me—an interpretation that
appears to have been lost for 1800 years.[1]

(3) Further, immediately after the seventh
Trumpet and the seventh Bowl, we hear what is
done, not on earth, but in heaven : in the former
instance, a song of thanksgiving, xi. 17 ; in the
latter, a voice from the temple and throne, saying,
"It is done," xvi. 17.   In like manner, immediately after the opening of the seventh Seal, what
took place in heaven should be recorded—*i.e.*
the silence enjoined on all the heavenly hosts,
an arrest of the praises and thanksgivings in
heaven, viii. 1, in order that the prayers of all
God's suffering servants on earth might be
heard before the throne of God, viii. 3–5.   In
vii. 1–3 there was an arrest of the judgments
on earth, until the faithful were sealed against

---

[1] This clause has proved an inscrutable enigma from the
earliest times. The most recent expositors have not been more
successful than the earlier. Swete says that this silence means
"a temporary suspension of revelation." Bousset interprets it
as expressing "an awful expectation of that which is to come."
Holtzmann expands this idea, and writes that in contrast to
the songs of praise that had continued from v. 9 to vii. 12
there followed a silence in heaven for the space of half an hour,
caused by the awful breathless expectation of the things that
were to come. Johannes Weiss and Porter express the same
idea in other words.

the coming plagues : here there is a further
and fresh pledge that the cause of the saints is
one with that of God, and of the heavenly
hosts.   It is worth observing that an analogous
idea is found in Judaism.   Thus in Chagiga
xii. 6, in the Talmud, we read that in the fifth
heaven are companies of angels of service who
sing praises by night, but are silent by day
" because of the glories of Israel," *i.e.* that the
praises of Israel may be heard in heaven.   This
passage supports our interpretation of the
enigmatic " silence in heaven," but it is far
less fine.   The idea in our text is infinitely
nobler.   The needs of the weakest saints on
earth concern God more than the psalmody of
the highest orders of the heavenly hosts.

*Original form and position of viii. 2 in
immediate connection with viii. 6, 12.*

viii. 2 is, then, an intrusion in its present
position and in its present form.   It probably
stood immediately after viii. 5 and together
with viii. 6 read as follows : " And I saw three
angels, and to them were given three trumpets.
And the three angels who had the three
trumpets prepared to sound."   Then, omitting
viii. 7–12, we should at once proceed to viii. 13
and read as follows : " And I saw, and heard
an eagle flying in the midst of heaven, saying

with a loud voice, Woe, woe, woe to them
that dwell on the earth because of the voices
of the trumpet of the three angels which are
about to sound."

Criticism of viii. 13.

In viii. 13, I wish you to observe that there
is only one word that calls for excision. This
is λοιπῶν = " the rest."

Now λοιπός is not used elsewhere in the
Apocalypse as an epithet. Together with the
article it forms a noun in eight passages
throughout the Apocalypse, in chaps. ii.–xx.
Moreover, its position before the noun is against
the usage of the writer with regard to epithets
in viii. 3–5, 13, ix. Epithets always follow
after the noun in these two chapters—in
sixteen cases. Thus λοιπῶν must be excised
as an interpolation. It is to be observed here
that the A.V. and the R.V. as well as some of
the earlier English versions add without any
authority the word "yet," and render "who
are yet to sound." This addition is quite
clearly owing to the fact that in the text as
it stands four trumpets have already been
mentioned. The added "yet" implies that
trumpets have already sounded. But the
Greek has no such implication : it is simply to
be rendered "which are about to sound." None

have sounded as yet. So far, then, for the criticism of this chapter. Adopting the conclusions we have now arrived at, I will read chap. viii. as it appears to have stood originally.

Chapter viii. in its original form.

1 " And when he opened the seventh seal, there followed a silence in heaven about the space of half an hour. 3 And an angel came and stood at the altar, with a golden censer ; and there was given to him much incense, that he should add it unto the prayers of all the saints upon the golden altar that was before the throne. 4 And the smoke of the incense, on behalf of the prayers of the saints, went up from the hand of the angel before God. 5 And the angel took the censer and filled it with the fire of the altar, and cast it upon the earth. And there followed thunders and voices, and lightnings and an earthquake.

2 And I saw three angels, and unto them were given three trumpets. 6 And the three angels who had the three trumpets prepared to sound. 13 And I saw, and I heard an eagle flying in the midst of heaven, saying with a loud voice, Woe, woe, woe, to them that dwell on the earth because of the voices of the trumpet of the three angels, which are about to sound."

Who is the angel in viii. 3? Michael or the
angel of peace?   Michael probably in the
original form of the chapter.

This, then, is all that we can assign of chap.
viii. to our author.   But before we leave the
above passage there are two questions that call
for consideration : who is the angel ? and what
is the altar ?   We can dispatch the first subject
quickly, if we eliminate the interpolations in
this chapter.   The angel was probably Michael,
as will appear presently.   But if we do not
eliminate the interpolations, the identification
of this angel is a matter of extreme difficulty ;
and yet it should not be so, seeing that it is
only one of the greatest angels who could be
entrusted with this function.   Let us take the
text as it stands, with the interpolations, and
investigate this question.   First of all, ver. 2
speaks of the seven angels who stand before
the throne of God.   Now, according to the
universal tradition of Judaism and early
Christianity, Michael was one of the foremost
of the seven archangels.   On the other hand,
according to Jewish tradition generally, it was
Michael that was the great intercessor on behalf of man.   Thus in 1 Enoch lxxxix. 76,
Michael prays on behalf of Israel ; and like
functions are presupposed in 1 Enoch lxviii.

3, 4. In this same work (xl. 9) he is called
"the merciful and longsuffering." According
to Rabbinic tradition, he offered sacrifices in
heaven, even the souls of the righteous ; and
like views prevailed in many early Christian
circles. Thus tradition points to the identification of this unnamed angel, who presents the
prayers of all the saints, with Michael.

But in the existing form of the text this angel,
who cannot be Michael, may be the angel
of peace.

But in the present interpolated form of the
text this cannot be right ; for, since Michael
is one of the seven angels mentioned in viii. 2,
he cannot at the same time be identical with
the other angel in viii. 3, who is so expressly
distinguished from the great Seven. It is
possible, therefore, that another tradition was
here followed by the interpolator, and even in
the original text. The "other angel" or "the
angel" may be the angel of peace referred to
in the Test. Dan vi. 5, whose office is "to
strengthen Israel, that it fall not into the
extremity of evil." In my notes to the Test.
Levi v. 6, 7, I have shown that these verses
most probably give a further description of this
angel who "intercedeth for the nation of Israel,
that they may not be smitten utterly," and

" for all the righteous." Again, in the Test.
Dan vi. 2 it is either Michael, or, as I am now
inclined to believe, this angel of peace, who is
described as the "mediator between God and
man," and who also "for the peace of Israel
shall stand up against the kingdom of the
enemy." Thus apparently similar functions
are ascribed to Michael and the angel of peace ;
for that they are not to be identified follows
from 1 Enoch xl. 8, 9, where they are clearly
distinguished. The nameless angel in Dan. x.
5–6, 12–14, 19–21, though generally identified
with Gabriel, may be this angel of peace. He
is an ally of Michael in helping Israel.

To sum up, then. The office of the angel
of peace was pre-eminently that of an intercessor
and mediator in Apocalyptic. He could,
therefore, in a Christian Apocalypse be
naturally assigned the duty of presenting the
prayers of the faithful before God. This great
angel is nameless in 1 Enoch, the Testaments
of the XII Patriarchs, and, if I am right in my
interpretation, also in Daniel. In our Apocalypse, too, he is nameless : he is simply
designated ἄλλος ἄγγελος in the present form
of the text, and was probably designated more
simply εἷς ἄγγελος in its original form. We
observe that though this angel is borrowed
from Judaism, he is not in any sense described

as mediating between God and His servants. He simply presents the prayers of the faithful, censing them as he presents them.

Were there two altars in the heavenly temple? Difficulties inherent in such a conception.

We now approach the next question, What is the altar at which the angel stands? We here enter on a very controverted subject. An altar in heaven is mentioned seven times in the Apocalypse. All commentators, so far as I am aware, assume the existence of two altars in the heavenly temple, and most commentators agree that the two altars—the altar of burnt-offering and the altar of incense — are referred to in our text. "And an angel came and stood at[1] the altar, with a golden censer; and there was given unto him much incense, that he should add it unto the prayers of all the saints upon the golden altar which was before the throne. And the smoke of the incense on behalf of the prayers of the saints went up from the hand of the angel before God. And the angel took the censer; and he filled it with the fire of the altar, and cast it upon the earth : and there followed thunders and voices, and lightnings, and an earthquake" (viii. 3–5).

---

[1] The text should be so translated, and not "over the altar"; cf. Amos ix. 1.

11

But if we assume a complete heavenly temple, with a holy place, a holy of holies, two altars, etc., we are forced to conclude either (1) with Züllig and Hengstenberg that the curtain of the holy of holies is closed in chap. iv. and viii. 3 sq. and not opened till xi. 19 ; or (2), with Hofmann, that the rest of the temple was removed in order to make possible the vision of God on His throne of Cherubin, and yet not that of the ark ; or (3) with Ebrard, that in the vision in chap. iv. the whole scene was disclosed without the temple, and that later in vi. 9, viii. 3 sqq., a heavenly temple appeared on a terrace below the height on which the throne stood ; or (4) with Bousset and Porter, that in chap. iv., vi. 7, viii. 3 sqq., the throne and the temple scenery are wholly irreconcilable.[1]

Now, unless I deceive myself, all these attempts at explanation proceed on a wrong hypothesis. We have here to do with the conceptions of the heavenly temple in *Apocalyptic*, and it is wholly unjustifiable to conclude that every characteristic part of the earthly temple has its prototype in the heavenly temple, as conceived in Apocalyptic. What we have now to do is to try and discover the conception of the heavenly temple that prevailed in Apoca-

[1] Yet this combination of the throne and temple scenery is as old as Isaiah's vision in Isa. vi.

lyptic Judaism. We have here entered on an interesting question in the history of religious development, which, however, we can on the present occasion only sketch in briefest outline.

The Vision of Isaiah vi. relates most probably to the earthly temple, but the Test. Levi to the heavenly. This conception arose between 300 and 150 B.C.

Our investigation starts with the vision of Isaiah in Isa. vi., since this passage has undoubtedly had a formative influence on subsequent developments, and was in the mind of the writer of the Apocalypse. I will quote the parts of this passage that concern us at present, vi. 1–8: "In the year that King Uzziah died I saw the Lord sitting upon a throne, high and lifted up, and the train of his vesture filled the temple. Above him stood the seraphim: each one had six wings; with twain he covered his face, and with twain he covered his feet, and with twain he did fly. And one cried unto another and said:

> Holy, holy, holy, is the Lord of Hosts,
> The whole earth is full of his glory.

And the foundations of the thresholds were moved at the voice of him that cried, and

the house began to fill with smoke. Then
said I :

> Woe is me ! for I am undone ;
> For a man of unclean lips am I,
> And in the midst of a people of unclean lips I dwell :
> For the King, the Lord of hosts, have mine eyes seen.

Then flew one of the seraphim unto me,
having a live coal in his hand, which he had
taken with the tongs from off the altar.
And he touched my mouth with it, and said :

> Lo, this hath touched thy lips :
> So thine iniquity shall depart,
> And thy sin be forgiven.

And I heard the voice of the Lord, saying :

> Whom shall I send,
> And who will go for us ? "

As Duhm, Cheyne, Marti, Whitehouse, and
Gray and other scholars have pointed out, the
temple and the altar referred to are those in
Jerusalem, as in the vision of Amos ix. 1 and
Ezek. viii. 3, x. 4. That the idea of a
heavenly temple and a heavenly altar existed
in pre-exilic times there is as yet no proof,
though such proof may some day be forth-
coming. On the other hand, we must conclude
from the Testament of Levi iii. 6, v. 1, xviii. 6,
that in the second century B.C. the idea of a
temple in heaven was current in certain circles,

and from the Apocalypse that it was a perfectly
familiar idea to the Christian Church in the
first century of our era.   Moreover, it is clear
from the diction that the authors of the
Testaments and of the Apocalypse had the
vision of Isa. vi. before them.   Thus in the
Testament Levi v. 1, the words, "the angel
opened to me the gate of heaven, and I saw
the holy temple, and upon a throne of glory
the Most High," clearly attest the influence
of Isaiah : "sitting upon a throne high and
lifted up, and the train of his vesture filled the
temple."   Again we might compare the Testament Levi xviii. 6 :

" And the heavens shall be opened,
  And from the temple of glory shall come upon him sancti-
      fication
  With the Father's voice as from Abraham to Isaac,"

with the voice from the temple in Isaiah.
Next, with the description in Isaiah we might
compare the temple in the Apocalypse being
filled with smoke in xv. 8, and the voice crying
from the temple in xvi. 1.

We have now seen that, on the one hand, in
the eighth century B.C. there was at first, so
far as we know, no idea of a heavenly temple
and a heavenly altar, while by the second
century B.C. this idea is firmly established.
But, furthermore, since it was unknown to

Ezekiel, the Priest's Code and the Chronicler,[1]
Dr. Buchanan Gray concludes that this
particular development took place between
500 and 100 B.C., and probably very consider-
ably nearer the latter than the earlier limit;
and in it we may see one of the early fruits
of that learned and speculative exegesis of the
Old Testament which is represented first in the
Apocalyptic literature and later in the various
Haggadic products of the Rabbinical Schools."[2]
This statement is undoubtedly good so far as
it goes, but alike the cause of the development
and the limits with which it actually arose can
probably be determined more exactly. The
determination of the probable limits of this
development depends on the cause from which
it sprung; and that this cause was the transference of the religious interest from earth to
heaven, which set in with the rise of the belief
in a blessed future life, is more than probable.
Indeed, on the emergence of this doctrine, ideas
in the Old Testament, which had a purely

[1] Gray appears to argue rightly that *tabnith* in Ezek. xliii.
10, Exod. xxv. 9, 40, 1 Chron. xxviii. 11–20, means not a model,
but a building plan. This plan was, according to 1 Chron.
xxviii. 19, received in writing by David from God, and passed
on by David to Solomon, xxviii. 11, 12. These references
taken in themselves do not postulate the belief in a heavenly
temple, as has frequently been urged.

[2] *Expositor*, 1908, pp. 385–402 530–546, and in his Commentary on Isa. vi. 1–4.

earthly reference, were in many cases transformed and given a heavenly significance. In
other words, they were reinterpreted from a
higher and spiritual standpoint. This process
of reinterpretation was for the most part
unconscious.[1]   On these grounds we may
reasonably conclude that this development
took place between 300 and 150 B.C.

If this principle is valid, we shall expect to
find it already at work in the latest books of
the Old Testament; and so, in fact, we do. I
have already given one instance in the last
lecture where it is pointed out that the book
of life meant in the Old Testament simply
a register of the citizens of the theocratic
community; and to have one's name written in
the book of life meant simply the right to
share in the *temporal* blessings of the Theocracy, while to be blotted out of this book
meant exclusion therefrom. In the Old
Testament this expression was originally confined to *temporal* blessings only, but in Dan.

---

[1] Such a process of reinterpretation would naturally be
fostered by the ideas underlying Exod. xxv. 9, 40, Num. viii. 4,
according to which the earthly altar and tabernacle were
made after the likeness of heavenly patterns. But these
passages were not the cause of the reinterpretation just
referred to : rather the reinterpretation of these passages was
due to the larger spiritual movement which transferred the
centre of interest from earth to heaven.

xii. 1 it is transformed through the writer's higher theology, and is distinctly conceived as referring to the blessed life of immortality.

Were there two altars or only one in the heavenly temple?

We have now dealt with the probable date of the emergence of the idea of a temple in heaven. That the idea of a heavenly altar arose about the same time may be reasonably concluded. But the problem is a complicated one. Were there two altars in this heavenly temple, or only one ? To answer this question we must carry our research back into the Old Testament and forward into Christian and Gnostic literature.

First, as regards the Old Testament, we shall simply state here the conclusions arrived at by Old Testament critics, that there was no altar of incense in the Tabernacle, nor in the temples of Solomon [1] and Ezekiel. In other words, down to the fifth century there is no reference to this altar, and the mention of this altar is assigned to a late stratum in the Priestly Code.[2] Thus originally there was only one altar in the Jewish temple, and that

---

[1] Exod. xxx. 10 and 1 Kings vii. 48 are late interpolations.
[2] See *Encyc. Bibl.* i. 126 sq. ; Hastings, *DB* ii. 467 sq., iv. 664 sq.

the altar of burnt-offering. But at some indeterminate date between the fifth century B.C. and 200 B.C.[1] the altar of incense was set up within the temple proper (ναός, היכל) and near the entrance to the holy of holies. There were thus in Herod's temple two altars—the altar of burnt-offering outside the porch of the temple, and the altar of incense inside the temple.

Two altars in the heavenly temple are said by scholars to be referred to in the Apocalypse.

Now it has hitherto been the universal opinion of scholars that as there were two altars in the earthly temple from the third or fourth century B.C. onward, so the heavenly temple was conceived by the Jews to have likewise two altars. Accordingly these two altars are said to be referred to in the Apocalypse.

But both Christian and Jewish evidence is against this view.

But, unless I am mistaken, this view appears to be wrong—at all events as regards Christian apocalyptic. First in Hermas, *Mand.* x. 3. 2, it is said : " The intercession of a sad man hath never power at any time to ascend to the altar

[1] See 1 Macc. i. 21, iv. 49 sq.

of God." Here clearly only one altar is presupposed; and that this altar is the altar of
incense is to be inferred from the fact that in
our Apocalypse (viii. 3) the prayers of the saints
are offered upon the golden altar before the
throne. This golden altar is, of course, recognised on all hands as the altar of incense.
"The altar" is again mentioned in *Sim.* viii.
2. 5; Irenæus also (iv. 18. 6) attests the same
view. He writes: "Thus (God) wishes us
also to offer gifts at the altar frequently
without intermission. There is therefore the[1]
altar in heaven (for thither our prayers and
oblations are directed), and the temple, as John
in the Apocalypse (xi. 19) says: "And the
Temple of God was opened, and the tabernacle "
(xxi. 3); for "Behold the tabernacle of God
in which he will dwell with men." Next we
find the following statement in the Apocalypse
of Paul, 44 (ed. Tischendorf): "And I saw
the four and twenty elders lying on their faces,
and I saw the altar and the throne." This

---

[1] Here only the Latin is preserved. The definite article,
however, is to be supplied before the three nouns *altar* ($= \tau \grave{o}$
$\theta υ σ ι α σ τ \acute{η} ρ ι ο ν$), *temple* ($= \acute{o}$ $ν α \acute{o} ς$), tabernaculum ($= \acute{η}$ $σ κ η ν \acute{η}$).
The Latin is: "Est ergo altare in cælis (illuc enim preces
nostræ et oblationes diriguntur), et templum, quemadmodum
Joannes in Apocalypsi ait: Et apertum est templum Dei; et
tabernaculum: Ecce enim, inquit, tabernaculum Dei in quo
habitabit cum hominibus."

altar is said to stand in the midst of the
heavenly city (29). Thus Primitive Christianity, so far as the above quotations go,
believed only in one altar in heaven ; and that
this altar was the altar of incense we learn
from Irenæus, who writes that it is to this altar
that our prayers and oblations are directed :
moreover, we have additional confirmation in
a Gnostic work of the second century, fragments of which are preserved by Clement of
Alexandria (iii. 437), where it is stated that
the soul "lays down its body near the altar
of incense, near the ministering angels of the
prayers that are offered."

Turning now to pre-Christian Judaism, we
see that only one altar is implied in the Test.
Levi iii. 6, where the archangels are described
as "offering to the Lord . . . a reasonable and
bloodless sacrifice." In later Judaism the same
view appears to prevail. According to Aboth
R. Nathan (second century A.D.), A. 26 (12),
the souls of the righteous rest under the
heavenly altar. Here there is only one altar
presupposed. Now, if we may take with this
statement another of the second century (R.
Eleazar's), found in Shabbath, 152^b, to the effect
that the souls of the righteous are preserved
under the throne of glory, we are justified in
concluding that the altar referred to is close

to the throne of God, and therefore within the heavenly temple. In any case, there is only one altar in question. In three other passages in the Talmud, statements are made to the effect that in the fourth heaven are to be found "Jerusalem and the temple and a built altar, and Michael the great prince standing and offering an offering thereon" (Chag. 2ᵇ, Zebach 62ᵃ, Menachoth (10ᵃ).

According to Christian literature of the second century A.D., and to Jewish literature of the same period and later, there was only one altar in heaven. Since this altar was in heaven, animal sacrifices could not be offered thereon, but only bloodless sacrifices and incense. Indeed, the nature of these sacrifices has, as we have seen, been defined in the Test. Levi iii. 6, "reasonable and bloodless" offerings, while later Judaism represents Michael as offering the souls of the departed righteous on this very altar.

There was originally only one altar in the earthly temple—an altar of burnt-offering, and never more than one altar—the altar of incense—in the heavenly temple in Jewish-Christian Apocalyptic outside the Apocalypse.

If the preceding account of the facts is trust-

worthy, we have now come to the interesting
conclusion that whereas there stood *in the
earthly temple* only one altar, the altar of
burnt-offering, down to the fifth century B.C.,
in the heavenly temple, on the other hand,
there stood only one altar, namely, the altar
of incense, according to Jewish and Christian
Apocalyptic from the second century B.C.
onwards, outside the Apocalypse.

It is now our task to inquire if this view
of the heavenly altar was held by the author
of the Apocalypse. Now, first of all, the fact
that Christian and Jew alike appear to have
held the same views as to the one altar in the
heavenly temple, proves of itself that this
belief was current in the first century in
Palestine before the breach of Christianity
with Judaism. Further, though no altar is
mentioned in the Test. Levi, which belongs to
the second century B.C., the text implies the
existence of only one altar.

We may therefore reasonably conclude that
in certain religious circles in Palestine this
conception of the heavenly altar was current
from the second century B.C. onwards.

A corollary that follows naturally, though
not inevitably, on this conclusion is that Jewish
mystics would be inclined to interpret, as in
fact they did, the great vision of Isa. vi. of the

heavenly temple.[1]   Amongst these mystics was
our Apocalyptist, who undeniably had Isa. vi.
before his mind in writing of the heavenly
temple.   Now, since in Isa. vi. there is only one
altar, we infer that in our Apocalyptist's view
there was only one altar likewise—in the latter
case the altar of incense.

It is worth observing in this connection that,
according to the apocalyptic school of the
higher theology, the altar of burnt-offering was
of small account as compared with the altar
of incense.   This we infer from 2 Bar. vi. 7-10,
according to which the earth was bidden by an
angel before the fall of Jerusalem to open and
receive certain sacred things belonging to the
temple, and to preserve them till the advent
of the Messianic Kingdom.   It is remarkable
that amongst these sacred things the altar of
incense is mentioned, but not the altar of burnt-
offering.

In another and wholly independent account
in 2 Macc. ii. 4–8, in which Jeremiah is bidden
by God to hide certain sacred things belonging
to the temple, the altar of incense is again

[1] Dr. Gray, indeed (*Expositor*, 1908, p. 504), is of opinion
that " Isaiah's vision, although it does not of itself refer to the
heavenly temple and altar, was a main cause in producing the
belief in them."   According to the view I have set forth, the
reinterpretation of Isaiah's vision would be only one example
of a principle at work affecting the entire Old Testament.

mentioned, but not the altar of burnt-offering.
This comparative depreciation of the altar
of burnt-offering was, no doubt, due to the
prophetic teaching, and to such Psalms as li.
15 sq.

15 "O Lord, open thou my lips ;
    And my mouth shall show forth thy praise.
16 For thou delightest not in sacrifice [that I should give
      it] ;
    Thou hast no pleasure in burnt-offering.
17 The sacrifices of God are a broken spirit :
    A broken and contrite heart, O God, thou wilt not
      despise."

*The Apocalypse does not, any more than Jew-
ish and Christian Apocalyptic outside
the Apocalypse, represent two altars as
the heavenly temple.*

We have now seen that Apocalyptic literature
in Judaism, both before and after the Christian
era, and in Christianity on to the second and
third centuries of this era, testifies to the existence of only one altar in heaven. We have
observed other facts indirectly leading to the
same conclusion. Armed with this knowledge,
let us now approach the Apocalypse and see if
the heavenly temple represented in it contains
two altars, as all scholars have hitherto held.

Let us deal first of all with chaps. viii. and ix.
Here there are universally assumed to be two

altars, one the altar of incense and the other
the altar of burnt-offering,—a conclusion that
is based on the hypothesis that the heavenly
temple is in every respect the heavenly original
after which the earthly temple was modelled,
and also on the fact that the altars are described in different terms. We have already
seen that the first reason is a groundless assumption in respect both to later Judaism and
Primitive Christianity, which presuppose only
one altar in the heavenly temple. As regards
the second reason, it is quite true that the
heavenly altar is designated in viii. 3*b* as " the
altar before the throne " (τὸ θυσιαστήριον τὸ
ἐνώπιον τοῦ θρόνου), and " the golden altar before
God " (τοῦ θυσιαστηρίου τοῦ χρυσοῦ τοῦ ἐνώπιον
τοῦ θεοῦ), in ix. 13. The altar so designated
is universally admitted to be the altar of
incense. This altar has already been presupposed, though not actually mentioned, in v. 8,
where the 24 Elders are described as having
harps and golden bowls full of incense. But
because this altar is simply called " the altar "
in viii. 3*a* and 5, it is declared that it must be
the altar of burnt-offering. There is no force
in this reason; for in Christian and Jewish
Apocalyptic literature the heavenly altar is
always designated as " the altar "; and this
altar was, as we have seen, the altar of incense.

The heavenly altar is referred to in only three other passages, vi. 9, xiv. 18, xvi. 7. In xiv. 18 the evidence points to the altar within the heavenly temple, *i.e.* the altar conceived as an altar of incense; for in xiv. 15, 17, the two preceding angels are said to come forth from the temple (ναός) "in heaven," and in xiv. 18 it is stated that "another angel went forth from the altar," the implication being that this altar is within the temple. There remain only vi. 9 and xvi. 7. xvi. 7 ("I heard the altar saying, True and righteous are thy judgments)" refers naturally to the altar on which the prayers of the saints were censed and offered, and which is described in ix. 13 as ordering the infliction of judgment, just as in xvi. 7 it is represented as vindicating the righteousness of God's judgment.

The altar in viii. is the altar of incense.

Only one passage now remains which has been regarded as furnishing incontestable evidence to the existence of an altar of burnt-offering in the heavenly temple, as well as an altar of incense. But there is not the slightest necessity for this supposition. According to Shabbath, 152ᵇ, the souls of the righteous are said by R. Eleazar in the second cent. A.D. to be preserved underneath the throne of God;

12

and, according to another authority of the same
period, to rest beneath the heavenly altar.
Hence this altar is close to, or beneath, the
throne of God, and must therefore be taken as
the altar of incense, since it is within the
heavenly temple, and is the only altar that is
within the heavenly temple.

*This altar has apparently some characteristics
belonging to the altar of burnt-offering.*

But this altar has the characteristics not
only of the altar of incense : *i.e.* it is close to
the throne of God, and within the heavenly
temple, and the prayers of the faithful are
offered thereon. It has also to some extent
the characteristics of the earthly altar of burnt-
offering; for the souls of the martyrs were
conceived as being offered thereon. With this
question I cannot deal further in these lectures,
but enough has been done to prove that in the
Apocalypse only one altar is conceived as standing in the heavenly temple, combining in itself
the characteristics of the altar of incense and to
some extent those of the altar of burnt-offering.

This idea of the offering of the souls of the
martyrs on the heavenly altar is implied in our
text, vi. 9 sqq., for the first time in literature.
The genesis of this idea can hardly be earlier
than the first cent. B.C. ; for before that period

the souls of the faithful were conceived as going directly to Hades at death and not to heaven, as in vi. 11 of the Apocalypse; but towards the close of the first cent. B.C. the belief that the soul ascends forthwith to heaven, is found in Philo, and later in 4 Maccabees, and probably in Wisdom.

The small interpolated Apocalypse, viii. 7–12. An attempt at its reconstruction.

I will conclude this chapter by giving a reconstruction of the short apocalypse, viii. 7, 12, which has been interpolated in our text. It was originally written in stanzas of five lines each.

viii. 7 :

" And the first angel sounded,
  And there followed hail and fire mingled with blood, and
    they were cast upon the earth :
  And the third part of the earth was burnt up,
  And the third part of the trees was burnt up,
  And the third part of the green grass."

viii. 8 :

" And the second angel sounded,
  And the likeness of a great mountain burning with fire
    was cast into the sea :
  And the third of the sun became blood ;
  And there died the third part of the creatures [1] that were
    in the sea ;
  And the third part of the ships were destroyed.

---

[1] In the third line of this stanza I have omitted as a gloss "which had life." It is a stupid gloss ; for how could the creatures "die," if they had not life to begin with ?

viii. 9 :

" And the third angel sounded,
  And there fell from heaven a great star, burning as a
      torch ;
  And it fell upon the third part of the rivers and springs."

viii. 11 :

" And the third part of the waters became like wormwood ;
  And the third part of mankind died of the waters."

Here I have omitted (as a gloss), " And the
name of the star is called Wormwood," which is
added after the third line of the stanza. It
obviously interrupts the close connection between line 3, " And it fell upon the third part
of the rivers and springs," and the fifth line,
" And the third part of the waters became wormwood." The construction, moreover, does not
occur again in the Apocalypse. And, finally,
the excision of this line restores the stanza to
its proper length. Further, as we have already
concluded (p. 148), the original read not, " And
many men died of the waters," but, " And the
third of mankind died of the waters," which I
have read accordingly.

We have now seen in the case of the first
three Trumpets that the text is verse and not
prose, and that in all probability each Trumpet
consisted of a stanza of five lines.

This fact leads us to expect in the fourth
Trumpet a stanza of five lines. Let us now

proceed to deal with this Trumpet. In the oldest MSS, ℵ A P and many cursives, it runs—

viii. 12 :

" And the fourth angel sounded,
  And the third of the sun was smitten,
  And the third of the moon, and the third of the stars;
  So that the third of them was darkened,
  And the day did not shine for a third of it, and the night likewise."

First of all, we remark how conventional this description is : how wholly wanting in imagination. A third again fails in every case. Again, how weak the cosmic catastrophes are, compared with those already described in vi. 12, where the entire sun is darkened and not the third part of it, as here ; where the whole moon becomes as blood, and where all the stars fall from heaven ; whereas here only a third of them is darkened. But this is not all. The last line is wholly unintelligible. There is no conceivable connection between the destruction of one-third of the light of the sun, and the shortening of the duration of the day by a third. Here the text is hopeless. If any meaning is to be extracted from this imbroglio, by "night" we are to understand "the moon and stars" which shine in the night. But this does not help matters.

Now in this verse we have followed the three
oldest Uncials, ℵ A P and Vg., *i.e. καὶ ἡ ἡμέρα
μὴ φάνῃ τὸ τρίτον αὐτῆς καὶ ἡ νὺξ ὁμοίως.* But
this text is not supported by the rest of the
MSS and Versions. Thus Q and very many
cursives give *καὶ τὸ τρίτον αὐτῆς μὴ φάνῃ ἡ
ἡμέρα καὶ ἡ νὺξ ὁμοίως,* "and that for the
third of it should not shine the day, and the
night likewise." Now we observe that there
is here no difference in the actual words used,
but there is a difference in the order. This
may seem a small matter, but it is not so.
Observe that the words "day and night" are
here brought together, as also in the Coptic
and Ethiopic Versions. This we shall find to
have been the primitive order. This is the first
step towards a solution of the difficulty. The
next step is that a considerable body of cursives
read *τὸ τρίτον αὐτῶν* instead of *τὸ τρίτον αὐτῆς.*
Here we have made the second step in the recovery of the original text, as I shall presently
show. But the remarkable feature about this
text is that it cannot be translated, whereas the
text in the Uncials can. Now it is hardly conceivable that scribes would deliberately change
a translatable, though unmeaning, text into
an untranslatable and likewise unmeaning text.
Hence I conclude that *τὸ τρίτον αὐτῶν μὴ φάνῃ
ἡ ἡμέρα* is in reality an older form than either

of the two former, though it is not attested
by any Greek MSS, earlier than the tenth
century.

It is, however, found in the Coptic Version.
Since this Version is assigned by most scholars
to the third or fourth century, this text appears
to be attested independently in the fourth
century.

Now let us return to the text again : καὶ τὸ
τρίτον αὐτῶν μὴ φάνῃ ἡ ἡμέρα καὶ ἡ νὺξ ὁμοίως. As
we examine this the true meaning of the text
flashes upon us. The subject of φάνῃ is τὸ τρίτον
αὐτῶν, " and the third of them shone not," and
not ἡ ἡμέρα καὶ ἡ νὺξ ὁμοίως. ἡ ἡμέρα καὶ ἡ νὺξ
ὁμοίως might be an early corruption for ἡμέρας
καὶ νυκτὸς ὁμοίως " by day and likewise by
night," which is not very likely, though the
Coptic Version attests this very reading, " and
the third of them shone not by day, nor likewise by night." Here we must conclude either
that the Coptic has preserved the original, or
that it recovered the original by a happy conjecture. I incline to the latter view. The text
is unintelligible in every Greek MS, and its
unintelligibleness is probably best explained by
a mistranslation of the Semitic original of the
Version, or owing to a corruption in the original.
If the original was Hebrew, the Hebrew may
have been ולא תאיר שלישיתם היום וכן גם הלילה. Here

היום and הלילה could be rendered either as ἡμέρας —νυκτός or ἡ ἡμέρα . . . ἡ νύξ.   In any case we should reconstruct the line as follows :

> "And the third of them shone not by day nor by night likewise."

APPENDIX TO CHAPTER II.

———◆———

THE CRITICAL ANALYSES OF SOME OF THE CHIEF STUDENTS OF THE APOCALYPSE DOWN TO RECENT TIMES.

———

Wherever the asterisk is attached to a verse it denotes a part of the verse; while *a, b, c,* etc., denote the first, second, or third clauses of the verse.

———

GROTIUS, *Annotationes in Apocalypsin Joannis,* 1644.— According to Grotius the Apocalypse consisted of ten visions experienced at different times and in different places. The first three visions (i.–xi.) belong to the reign of Claudius, visions four and five (xii.–xiv.) before the fall of Jerusalem (?), visions six and seven (xv.–xviii.) to the reign of Vespasian, visions eight to ten (xix.–xxii.) to that of Domitian.

VÖLTER.—Völter's first work appeared in 1882, but since he has seriously modified the views in that work in his three subsequent studies, only his latest views are here given in *Die Offenbarung Johannis*, 1904.

Apoc. of John Mark.[1] 60 A.D.	Apoc. of Cerinthus. 70 A.D.	Editor in Trajan's Time. 114-115 A.D.	Revises in Hadrian's Time.
i. 4–6.	x. 1–11.	i. 7–8.	i. 1–3, 9–iii.
iv. 1–v. 10.	xvii. 1–18.	v. 6b, 9–10*.	22.
vi. 1–vii. 8.	xi. 1–13.	v. 11–14.	xiv. 13.
viii.–ix.	xii. 1–16.	vii. 9–17.	xvi. 15.
xi. 14–19.	xv. 5–6, 8.	xi. 8*, 11*, 15*, 18*.	xix. 10b.
xiv. 1–3, 6–7.	xvi.	xii. 11, 18–xiii. 18.	xxii. 7, 10–
xviii. 1–xix. 4.	xix. 11–xxi. 8.	xiv. 4–5, 9–12.	20.
xiv. 14–20.	xxi. 10–xxii.	xv. 1–4, 7.	
xix. 5–10a.	6.	xvi. 2b (13), 19b.	
		xvii. 6*, 14, 16, 17.	
		Phrases in xix. 20,	
		xx. 10	
		xxi. 14, 22–27.	
		xxii. 1–2, 8–9.	

VISCHER, *Die Offenbarung Johannis*, 1886.—According to Vischer the groundwork of the Apocalypse is a Jewish work. This was revised by a Christian to whom the following additions are due:

i.–iii.	xi. 15*.	xvii. 14.
v. 6*.	xii. 11, 17 (a word).	xviii. 20*.
v. 8 (a word).	xiii. 8*.	xix. 7*.
v. 9–14.	xiii. 9–10.	xix. 9–10.
vi. 1*.	xiv. 1–5.	xix. 11*.
vi. 16*.	xiv. 10*.	xix. 13b.
vii. 9–17.	xiv. 12–13.	xx. 4–5*, 6.
ix. 11*.	xv. 3*.	xxi. 5b–8, 9*, 14b,
xi. 8b, c.	xvi. 15, 16*.	22*, 23*, 27*.
	xvii. 6*.	xxii. 3*, 6–21.

[1] See *Offenbarung Johannis*, pp. 51, 59, 61, 62, 70, 71, 98, 104–7, 145–7. Interpolations in individual verses of the Apoc. of John, Völter detects in iv. 1, v. 9, 10, vi. 16, xi. 8, 11, 15, 18, xiv. 1, xviii. 20; in the Apoc. of Cerinthus x. 6b, 7b, xi. 8, xvi. 2, 3, xvii. 1, xix. 20, xx. 4, 10, xxi. 9, xxii. 3.

Schoen, *L'Origine de l'Apocalypse de Saint Jean*, 1887.—According to this writer the main elements of the Apocalypse are Christian (see pp. 137–139).

Christian Apocalypse written under Domitian.	Christian Editor.	Jewish Sources.
i.–ix.	x.	xi. 1–13.
xi. 14, 15.	xii. 10–12, 18.	xii.
xiv. 1–8, 13–20.	xiii. 8–10.	xiii.
xv.–xvi.	xiv. 9–12.	xviii.
xix.–xx.	xvi. 13–16.	
xxi. 1–8.	xvii.	
xxii. 6–21.	xviii. 20.	
	xix.	
	xx. 1–6, 7–15.	
	xxi. 9–xxii. 5.	

Weyland, *Omwerkings-en Compilatie-Hypothesen toegepast op de Apocalypse van Johannes*, 1888.—Weyland discovers two Jewish sources in the Apocalypse א and ב. These two sources were edited by a Christian, who added the first three chapters and a series of interpolations (see p. 176).[1]

א (Written under Titus.)	ב (Written under Nero.)	Christian Editor.[1]
i. 10, 12–17, 19.	x. 1–xi. 13.	i.–iii.
iv.–vi.	xii. 1–10, 11–xiii.	iv. 5c.
vii. 1–8, 9–17.	xiv. 6–7, 9–11.	v. 6–14 (recast).
viii.–ix.	xv. 2–4.	vi. 16c.
xi. 14–18.	xvi. 13, 14.	vii. 14c.
xiv. 2–3.	xix. 11–21.	ix. 18.
xiv. 14–20.	xx.	x. 7.
xv. 5.	xxi. 1–8.	xi. 8b.
xvi. 17b–20.		xii. 11, 17c.
xvii.–xix. 6.		xiv. 1, 4–5, 12–13.
xxi. 9–27.		xv. 1, 6–8.
xxii. 1–11, 14–15.		xvi. 1–17a, 21.
		xvii. 14.
		xix. 7–10, 13b.
		xxi. 9a, 14b.
		xxii. 7a, 12–13, 16–21.

[1] Also words and phrases in vi. 1, vii. 9, 10, 17, ix. 15, x. 1, 11, xiii. 8, xv. 3, xvii. 6, xviii. 20, xx. 4, xxi. 27, xxii. 1, 3.

SPITTA, *Die Offenbarung des Johannes*, 1889.—According to Spitta there was a primitive Christian Apocalypse, U, written soon after 60 A.D. This was revised by a Christian editor R in the time of Trajan, who incorporated two Jewish Apocalypses, J¹ belonging to the time of Caligula, and J² to that of Pompey.

U.	J¹.	J².	R.
i. 4-6, 9-19.	vii. 1-8.	x. 1b, 2a, 8a, 9b, 10-11.	i. 1-3.
ii. 1-6, 8-10, 12-16, 18-25.	viii. 2-ix. 14, 15b.	xi. 1-13, 15, 17, 18.	i. 5*.
iii. 1-4, 7-11, 14-20.	viii. 16-21, 15a,	xiv. 14-20.	i. 7-8, 20.
iv.-vi.	x. 1a, 2b, 3, 5-7.	xv. 2-6, 8.	ii. 7, 11, 17, 26-29.
vii. 9-17.	xi. 15, 19.	xvi. 1-12, 17a, 21.	iii. 5-6, 12-13, 21-22.
viii. 1.	xii.-xiii. 8.	xvii. 1-6a.	iv. 1".
xix. 9b, 10.	xiii. 11-18.	xviii. 1-23.	v. 5*, 6*, 9*, 10*.
xxii. 8, 10-13, 16a, 17, 18a, 20b-21.	xiv. 1-2a, 4b-7, 9, 10b, 11a.	xix. 1-8.	vi. 16*.
	xvi. 13, 14, 17b-20.	xxi. 9-xxii. 3a, 15.	vii. 9c.
	xix. 11-21.		ix. 12, 14*, 15*.
	xx. 1-3, 8-15.		x. 4, 5*, 7a.
	xxi. 1, 5a, 6a.		xi. 14.
			xii. 6, 9*, 11, 13*, 17*.
			xiii. 3a, 4b, 5b, 7a, 8*, 9-10, 14*, 17c-18abc.
			xiv. 2b-4a, 4b*, 6*, 8, 10a, 11a, 11c-13, 17.
			xv. 1, 2*, 3*, 5b, 7.
			xvi. 1*, 2*, 10*, 15.
			xvii. 3*, 6a, 7-18.
			xviii. 24.
			xix. 4, 6*, 7*, 8b-9a, 10*, 11d-12a, 13b, 15, 21*.
			xx. 2*, 4-7, 12*.
			xxi. 2-4, 5b, 6b-8, 9*, 14*, 22*, 23*, 27b.
			xxii. 1*, 3b-7, 14, 16b, 18b-20a.

ERBES, *Die Offenbarung Johannis*, 1891.—Erbes' theory is that of the Redaction Hypothesis. The groundwork consists of a Christian Apocalypse written in the year 62 A.D. With this Apocalypse another of the time of Caligula was incorporated, and finally about the year 80 it was finally revised and enlarged. See p. 184.

Caligula Apoc. 40 A.D.	Christian Apoc. 62 A.D.	Final Redaction. 80 A.D.
xii. 1–xiii. 18. xiv. 9*b*–12.	i. 4–19. ii. 1–6, 8–10, 12–16, 18–25. iii. 1–4, 7–11, 14–22. iv. 1–5, 10. v. 1–10 (11–14). vi. vii. 1–3, 9–12. viii. 1–11, 19. xiv. 1–7, 13–20. xv. 2*–4 (v. 11–14). xix. 5–9*a*. xx. 11–15. xxi. 1–4. xxii. 3–25.	i. 1–3, 20. ii. 7, 11, 17, 26–29. iii. 5–6, 12–13. vii. 4–8, 13–17. ix. 12. xi. 14. xiii. 3*, 12*, 14*. xiv. 4*, 8, 9*a*. xv. 1, 2*, 5–xix. 4. xix. 9*b*–xx. 10, 14*. xxi. 5–xxii. 2. (xxii. 18, 19 ?)

J. WEISS, *Die Offenbarung des Johannes*, 1908.—According to Weiss there was an original Johannine Apocalypse written probably before 70 A.D. This Apocalypse was re-edited in 95 A.D. by a writer who at the same time incorporated an anonymous Apocalypse written before 70 A.D.

Apocalypse of John.	Anonymous Apoc. Q.	Editor, 95 A.D.
i. 4–6, 9–15, 17. ii.1–5, 8–10, 12–16. ii. 18–25. iii. 1–4, 7–11, 14–20. iv. 1–8 (with the exception of some phrases). v. 1–6*a*, 7–8, 11–14. vi. 1–8, 12–17. vii. 1–8 (H). viii. 1, 3–5*a*, 13–ix. 21. xi. 14. xii. 7–12. xiv. 1–7, 14–20. xx. 1–4*a*, 6–11. xxi. 1–4*. xxii. 3–5 (8–9).	x. 1–9. xi. 1–13. xii. 1–6, 13–17. xiii. 1–2*a*, 3–6. xv. 5, 8–xvi. 1. xvii. 1–8, 9*b*–13, 15–18. xviii. 1–19. xix. 11–21. xxi. 9–xxii. 2.	i. 1–3, 7–8, 16 (?), 19 (?)–20. ii. 6 (?), 7, 10*e*–11, 17, 26–29. iii. 5–6, 12–13, 21–22. iv. 5*b*, 9–11. v. 6*, 8*. vi. 9–11. vii. 9–17 (J). viii. 2, 5*b*–12. x. 7*, 10–11. xi. 8*, 15. xii. 3*, 11. xiii. 2*b*, 7–10, 11–18 (J). xiv. 8–12. xv. 1–4, 6, 7. xvii. 9*a*, 14. xviii. 20. xix. 1–10. xx. 4*b*–5, 12*b*–15. xxi. 4*–8, 14. xxii. 6–7, 10–21.

I have not given the analyses of Bousset, Wellhausen, and Moffatt, which in the opinion of the present writer adopt other methods for dealing with the Apocalypse. With these scholars I hope to deal in my Commentary next year.

INDEX I.

NAMES OF COMMENTATORS ON THE APOCALYPSE.

INDEX II.

———◆———

SUBJECTS.

ABADDON, 102.
Abbott, *Johannine Grammar*, 90, 148.
Aboth d. R. Nathan, 171.
Acts of Thomas, 127.
Albigenses, massacre of, 22.
Alexandrian school, 9, 10. See Interpretation, allegorical method of.
Allegory in the Apocalypse, 6, 9.
Altar in heaven, 161–179 ; one only in primitive Christianity, 169, 171 ; in pre-Christian Judaism, 171, 172. See Temple.
   of burnt-offering, in earthly temple, 169, 173.
   of incense, a later development, in earthly temple, 168–169 ; but of higher value, 174 ; as being the heavenly altar, 177–179.
Angel, of peace, 159–161.
   with golden censer, = Michael or angel of peace, 158–161.
Angels, of the four winds, 111.
   of waters and of fire, 112.
   seven, before the throne of God, = Archangels, 158.
Antichrist, 6, 10, 14, 17 n., 117, 130, 144 ; from Dan, 10, 114–117 ; in future, 33, = Nero redivivus, 46, 47,

= papacy. See Papacy, = Saracens, 24 ; tradition of, 9, 117. See Mystery of wickedness.
Antiochus Epiphanes, 6.
Anti-papal bias, 30, 31, 36, 54–55. See Papacy.
Apocalypse, the, author of, a Christian prophet addressing his contemporaries, various views as to identity :—Cerinthus, 60, John Mark, 60 ; John Chrysostom, 53, 54.
   character of, Christian, 60, 65, 68 ; Jewish, 61 63, 65, 66, 73.
   composition of, theories of, 42, 58–75—fragment, 72 75 ; redactional, 59–68 ; sources, 68–71.
   date of, 53, 57, 59–61, 109.
   dates and numbers in, 9, 10, 15–17, 20, 21, 24, 26, 35, 39–40, 41, 43, 44. See Chronologisings.
   diction of, 108.
   elements in, Jewish, 65, 73, 74, 111, 155, 158, 163, 167, 174 ; and Christian, 65, 73 ; non-Jewish, (ethnic), 76. See Book of Life, Sealing.

Dates and Numbers. See Apocalypse.
Demonic dangers in last days, 129.
Dominicans. See Franciscans.
Domitian, 35, 41, 57 n.
Dragon, 69 ; an Apollyon, 102, = heathen priesthood of Asia Minor, 100. See Beast, second.

Eleazar, Rabbi, 171, 177.
End of world expected, 14 ; time of, 144 n.
Enoch, 1 Book of, 58, 112, 158, 159, 160.
Essenes, 64.
Eternal Gospel, = Joachim's writings, 20, — Luther's teaching, 28.
Evil, final annihilation of, 144 n.

Feet = legs, 97, 98.
Franciscans and Dominicans, and Joachim's prophecies, 19, 20.
Frederick II., 19, 20, 24. See Gregory.

Gentile Christians, 107, 133–136.
Gog and Magog, = Turks, and Luther, 29.
Grammar. See Apocalypse.
Gregory IX. and Frederick II., 24.

Hadrian, 60.
Heavenly altar—of incense, 177–179. See Altar.
  patterns, 166–167 notes.
  temple. See Temple.
Hebraisms, 71, 79–102.
Helvetic Confession, denounces Chiliasm, 30, 31.
Hermas, 169–170.
Honorius III., 17 n.

Innocent III., 22, 24.
Interpolations, 151–154, 156.

Interpretation, methods of—
  i. Allegorical or spiritualising, 11–12, 25, 33.
    (a) combined with Recapitulation theory, 12.
    (b) purely abstract, 13, 25 ; effect of, on Church, 26. See vi. (a).
  ii. Astronomical, 50–54.
  iii. Chiliastic, extravagant developments of, 36–40 ; flourishes in England, 31, 38. See iv., vi. (b), viii., also under Chiliasm.
  iv. Eschatological, 4, 5, 7–11, 30, 32, 55–56 ; in a form involving Chiliasm and the Recapitulation method, 15–17 ; in parts preserved in tradition, 8 ; revived by Jesuit scholars, 32–36.
  v. Literary-Critical, 7 ; rise of, in seventeenth century, 36, 40–43 ; three hypotheses possible in, 58–74.
  vi. Historical—
    (a) Church, 27–30, 43, 55, 56.
    (b) Contemporary, 4, 5, 7, 8, 10, 11, 25, 30, 32–37, 41 ; early lost, 8 ; revived by Jesuit scholars, 33–36 ; recovered by Bibliander and Grotius, 40–42 ; at last asserted in limited and perverse form, 43–46 ; in full and legitimate form, 56, 57 ; with or without Chiliastic interpretation, 46–49.
    (c) Religious, 7.
    (d) Symbolical, 54, 55, 56.
    (e) Traditional, 7. See Tradition.
    (f) World, 30, 33, 37, 41, 43, 54–56.
  vii. Philological, 7, 32.

200

Printed by
MORRISON & GIBB LIMITED
Edinburgh

L

THE PUBLICATIONS OF
T. & T. CLARK

38 GEORGE STREET, EDINBURGH.
STATIONERS' HALL, LONDON.

* *A full detailed Catalogue may be had on application.*

Abbott (Prof. T. K.). EPHESIANS AND COLOSSIANS. (*International Critical Commentary.*) **10/6.**

Adam (Dr. James). THE RELIGIOUS TEACHERS OF GREECE. Edited, with a Memoir, by his WIFE. Second Edition, **10/6 net.**

Adams (Prof. John). PRIMER ON TEACHING, with special reference to Sunday School Work. **6d. net.**

Adams (Rev. John). SERMONS IN ACCENTS ; or, Studies in the Hebrew Text. **4/6 net.**

—— SERMONS IN SYNTAX. **4/6 net.**

—— ISRAEL'S IDEAL : Studies in Old Testament Theology. **4/6 net.**

—— THE LENTEN PSALMS. (*Short Course Series.*) **2/– net.**

—— THE MAN AMONG THE MYRTLES : A Study in Zechariah's Visions. (*Short Course Series.*) **2/– net.**

Adamson (Rev. R. M.). THE CHRISTIAN DOCTRINE OF THE LORD'S SUPPER. **4/6 net.**

Adeney (Principal W. F., D.D.). THE GREEK AND EASTERN CHURCHES. (*International Theological Library.*) **12/–.**

Agnew (Rev. Joseph). LIFE'S CHRIST PLACES. **3/6 net.**

Allen (Prof. A. V. G.). CHRISTIAN INSTITUTIONS. (*International Theological Library.*) **12/–.**

Allen (Willoughby C., M.A.). ST. MATTHEW. (*International Critical Commentary.*) Third Edition, **12/–.**

Andrews (Rev. S. J.). THE LIFE OF OUR LORD. Revised Ed., **9/–.**

Ante-Nicene Christian Library. A COLLECTION OF ALL THE WORKS OF THE FATHERS OF THE CHRISTIAN CHURCH PRIOR TO THE COUNCIL OF NICÆA. Twenty-four vols., Subscription price, £6, 6/–. Selection of any Four Volumes, 21/– net. Single vols., **10/6.**

—— RECENTLY DISCOVERED MSS. (Additional Volume). **12/6 net.**

Astley (Dr. H. J. D.). PREHISTORIC ARCHÆOLOGY AND THE OLD TESTAMENT. **5/– net.**

Augustine's Works. Edited by MARCUS DODS, D.D. 15 vols., Subscription price, £3, 19/– net. Selection of any Four Vols., 21/– net. Single vols., **10/6.**

Bain (Rev. John A.). THE NEW REFORMATION. Second Edition, **4/6 net.**

Ball (W. E., LL.D.). ST. PAUL AND THE ROMAN LAW. **4/6.**

Ballar (Dr. Frank). THE MIRACLES OF UNBELIEF. Seventh Edition, **2/6 net.**

Barry (Rev. J. C.). IDEALS AND PRINCIPLES OF CHURCH REFORM. **3/– net.**

Bartlet (Prof. J. Vernon). THE APOSTOLIC AGE : ITS LIFE, DOCTRINE, WORSHIP, AND POLITY. (*Eras of Church History.*) **6/–.**

Barton (Prof. G. A.). ECCLESIASTES. (*International Critical Commentary.*) **8/6.**

Bayne (P., LL.D.). THE FREE CHURCH OF SCOTLAND. **3/6.**

Beck (Prof. J. T.). OUTLINES OF BIBLICAL PSYCHOLOGY. **4/–.**

—— PASTORAL THEOLOGY OF THE NEW TESTAMENT. **6/–.**

Bennett (Prof. W. H.). THE RELIGION OF THE POST-EXILIC
PROPHETS.　　　　　　　　　　　　　　　　　　**6/- net.**
———— THE MOABITE STONE.　　　　　　　　　　**2/6 net.**

Beveridge (Rev. W.). A SHORT HISTORY OF THE WESTMINSTER
ASSEMBLY.　　　　　　　　　　　　　　　　　　**2/6 net.**

Beyschlag (Prof. W.). NEW TESTAMENT THEOLOGY. Two vols.
　　　　　　　　　　　　　　　　　Second Edition, **18/- net.**

Bible Class Handbooks. Fifty-three vols. ready, 1/3 to 3/- each.
Edited by Principal ALEXANDER WHYTE, D.D., and Rev. JOHN KELMAN,
D.D. (*See page* 15.)

Bible Class Primers. Forty-six now issued in the Series.
Edited by Principal S. D. F. SALMOND, D.D. (*See page* 15.)
　　　　　Paper covers, **6d.** each; by post, **7d.** In cloth, **8d.**; by post, **9d.**

Bible Dictionary—IN ONE VOLUME. Edited by Dr. HASTINGS.
(*See page* 16.)
———— IN FIVE VOLUMES. Edited by Dr. HASTINGS. (*See page* 16.)

Bigg (Prof. Chas.). ST. PETER AND ST. JUDE. (*International
Critical Commentary.*)　　　　　　　　　Second Edition, **10/6.**

Blake (Rev. Buchanan). HOW TO READ THE PROPHETS. The
Pre-Exilian Minor Prophets (with Joel), Second Edition, **4/-**; Isaiah (ch.
i.-xxxix., Third Edition, **2/6**; Ezekiel, **4/-**; Isaiah (ch. xl.-lxvi.), and
Post-Exilian Prophets, **4/-**; Joseph and Moses: Founders of Israel, **4/-**.
Messrs. Clark now offer this Set of Five Volumes for 15/-.

Bliss (Dr. F. J.). THE RELIGIONS OF MODERN SYRIA AND
PALESTINE.　　　　　　　　　　　　　　　　**4/6 net.**

Blunt (Rev. A. W. F.). FAITH AND THE NEW TESTAMENT. **2/- net.**

Briggs (Prof. C. A.). GENERAL INTRODUCTION TO THE STUDY
OF HOLY SCRIPTURE.　　　　　　　　　　　　**12/- net.**
———— PSALMS. (*International Critical Commentary.*)
　　　　　　　　　　　　　　　　Two vols., **10/6** each.
———— THE MESSIAH OF THE APOSTLES.　　　　**7/6.**
———— THE MESSIAH OF THE GOSPELS.　　　　　**6/6.**

Brockelmann (C.). LEXICON SYRIACUM. With a Preface by
Professor T. NÖLDEKE.　　　　　　　　　Crown 4to, **30/- net.**

Brockington (Rev. A. Allen). OLD TESTAMENT MIRACLES IN
THE LIGHT OF THE GOSPEL.　　　　　　　　　**3/- net.**

Brooke (Rev. A. E.). THE JOHANNINE EPISTLES. (*International
Critical Commentary.*)　　　　　　　　　　　　**10/6.**

Brown (Prof. W. Adams). THE ESSENCE OF CHRISTIANITY.
　　　　　　　　　　　　　　　　　　　　　6/- net.
———— CHRISTIAN THEOLOGY IN OUTLINE.　　　**7/6 net.**

Bruce (Prof. A. B.). THE TRAINING OF THE TWELVE; exhibit-
ing the Twelve Disciples under Discipline for the Apostleship.
　　　　　　　　　　　　　　　　　Sixth Edition, **10/6.**
———— THE HUMILIATION OF CHRIST.　　Fifth Edition, **10/6.**
———— THE KINGDOM OF GOD; or, Christ's Teaching according to the
Synoptical Gospels.　　　　　　　　　　　　　**7/6.**
———— APOLOGETICS; OR, CHRISTIANITY DEFENSIVELY STATED.
(*International Theological Library.*)　　　Third Edition, **10/6.**
———— ST. PAUL'S CONCEPTION OF CHRISTIANITY.　　**7/6.**
———— THE EPISTLE TO THE HEBREWS: The First Apology for
Christianity.　　　　　　　　　　　　Second Edition, **7/6.**

Bruce (Dr. Robert). APOSTOLIC ORDER AND UNITY. **2/6 net.**

Bruce (Dr. W. S.). THE ETHICS OF THE OLD TESTAMENT.
　　　　　　　　　　　　　　　　　Second Edition, **4/-.**
———— THE FORMATION OF CHRISTIAN CHARACTER. Second Edition, **5/-.**

Burkitt (Prof. F. C.). THE GOSPEL HISTORY AND ITS TRANS-
MISSION.　　　　　　　　　　　　　Third Edition, **6/- net.**

Bussell (Vice-Principal F. W.). Marcus Aurelius and the Later Stoics. 3/-.

Caldecott (Prof. A.) and Mackintosh (Prof. H. R.). Selections from the Literature of Theism. Second Edition, 7/6 net.

Calvin's Commentaries. Forty-five vols. *Price on application.*

Calvin's Institutes of Christian Religion. (Translation.) 2 vols. 14/-.

Calvini Institutio Christianæ Religionis. Curavit A. Tholuck. Two vols. 14/- net.

Candlish (Prof. J. S.). The Kingdom of God, Biblically and Historically considered. 10/6.

———— The Christian Salvation. Lectures on the Work of Christ. 7/6.

Carrick (Rev. J. C.). Wycliffe and the Lollards. 3/-.

Cave (Principal Alfred). The Scriptural Doctrine of Sacrifice and Atonement. Second Edition, 10/6.

———— An Introduction to Theology. Second Edition, 12/-.

Chadwick (Dr. W. E.). The Pastoral Teaching of St. Paul. His Ministerial Ideals. 7/6 net.

Chapman (Principal C.). Pre-Organic Evolution and the Biblical Idea of God. 6/-.

Christ and the Gospels, Dictionary of. Edited by Dr. Hastings. *(See page 16.)*

Christlieb (Prof. T.). Modern Doubt and Christian Belief. 6/- net.

———— Homiletic: Lectures on Preaching. 7/6.

Clark (Prof. W. R.). The Anglican Reformation. (*Eras of Church History.*) 6/-.

———— Pascal and the Port Royalists. 3/-.

———— Witnesses to Christ. 4/-.

Clarke (Professor W. N., D.D.). The Christian Doctrine of God. (*International Theological Library.*) 10/6.

———— An Outline of Christian Theology. Twentieth Edition, 7/6.

———— The Ideal of Jesus. 5/- net.

———— Sixty Years with the Bible: A Record of Experience. 4/6 net.

———— The Use of the Scriptures in Theology. 4/-.

———— What shall we think of Christianity? 2/6.

———— Can I believe in God the Father? 3/-.

Clemen (Prof. Carl). Primitive Christianity and its Non-Jewish Sources. 9/- net.

Clifford (Dr. John). The Gospel of Gladness. 4/6 net.

Coats (Rev. R. H.). Types of English Piety. 4/- net.

Concordance to the Greek Testament. Moulton (W. F.) and Geden (Prof. A. S.). Third Edition. Crown 4to, 26/- net.

Cooke (Canon G. A.). The Progress of Revelation. 4/6 net.

Cooper (Prof. James) and MacLean (Bishop A. J.). The Testament of our Lord. With Introduction and Notes. 9/-.

Cremer (Professor). Biblico-Theological Lexicon of New Testament Greek. Third Edition, with Supplement, demy 4to, 38/-.

Crippen (Rev. T. G.). A Popular Introduction to the History of Christian Doctrine. 9/-.

Curtis (Prof. Edward L.). The Books of Chronicles. (*International Critical Commentary.*) 12/-.

Curtis (Prof. W. A.). A History of Creeds and Confessions of Faith in Christendom and Beyond.   10/6 net.

Dahle (Bishop). Life after Death.   10/6.

Dalman (Prof. G.). The Words of Jesus.   7/6 net.

Davidson (Prof. A. B.). An Introductory Hebrew Grammar. With Progressive Exercises in Reading and Writing.   Eighteenth Edition, 7/6.

———— Hebrew Syntax.   Third Edition, 7/6.

———— Old Testament Prophecy.   10/6 net.

———— The Theology of the Old Testament. (*International Theological Library.*)   12/-.

———— The Called of God. With Biographical Introduction by A. Taylor Innes, LL.D., and Portraits.   Second Edition, 6/-.

———— Waiting upon God. A Further and Final Selection of Sermons.   6/-.

———— The Epistle to the Hebrews.   2/6.

Davidson (Dr. Samuel). Autobiography and Diary. Edited by his Daughter.   7/6.

Davidson (Prof. W. L.). The Stoic Creed.   4/6 net.

Davies (Principal D. C.). The Atonement and Intercession of Christ.   4/-.

Dean (Rev. John T.). Visions and Revelations.   5/- net.

Deane (Wm., M.A.). Pseudepigrapha: The Books which influenced our Lord and the Apostles.   7/6.

Deissmann (Dr. Adolf). Bible Studies.   Second Edition, 9/-.

———— New Light on the New Testament.   3/- net.

Delitzsch (Prof.). System of Biblical Psychology.   6/- net. New Commentary on Genesis, 2 vols. 12/- net; Psalms, 3 vols., 18/- net; Proverbs, 2 vols., 12/- net; Song of Solomon and Ecclesiastes, 6/- net; Isaiah, Fourth Edition, 2 vols., 12/- net; Hebrews, 2 vols., 12/- net.

*** Any Four Volumes may be had at original Subscription price of 21/- net.

Deussen (Prof. P.). The Philosophy of the Upanishads. The Religion and Philosophy of India.   10/6.

Dictionary of the Bible. Edited by Dr. Hastings. (*See page* 16.)

Dictionary of Christ and the Gospels. Edited by Dr. Hastings. (*See page* 16.)

Dods (Principal Marcus). The Bible: Its Origin and Nature.   4/6 net.

Dods (Marcus, M.A.). Forerunners of Dante.   4/- net.

Döllinger (Dr. I. von). Declarations and Letters on the Vatican Decrees, 1869-1887.   3/6.

Dorner (Prof. I. A.). History of the Development of the Doctrine of the Person of Christ. Five vols. Subscription price, 26/3 net.

———— System of Christian Doctrine. Four vols.   Subscription price, 21/- net.

———— System of Christian Ethics.   14/-.

Downer (Dr. A. C.). The Mission and Ministration of the Holy Spirit.   7/6 net.

Driver (Prof. S. R.). An Introduction to the Literature of the Old Testament. (*International Theological Library.*)   Eighth Edition, 12/-.

———— Deuteronomy. (*International Critical Commentary*).   Third Edition, 12/-.

Drummond (Dr. R. J.). The Relation of the Apostolic Teaching to the Teaching of Christ.   Second Edition, 10/6.

Du Bose (Prof. W. P.). The Ecumenical Councils. (*Eras of Church History.*)   6/-.

Dudden (Dr. F. Homes). CHRIST AND CHRIST'S RELIGION. 4/6 net.
Duff (Prof. David). THE EARLY CHURCH. 12/-.
Durell (Rev. J. C. V.). THE SELF-REVELATION OF OUR LORD.
5/- net.
Dyke (Paul Van). THE AGE OF THE RENASCENCE. With an
Introduction by HENRY VAN DYKE. (*Eras of Church History.*) 6/-.
Dykes (Principal J. Oswald). THE CHRISTIAN MINISTER AND
HIS DUTIES. 6/- net.
——— THE DIVINE WORKER IN CREATION AND PROVIDENCE. 6/- net.
Eadie (Professor). COMMENTARIES ON ST. PAUL'S EPISTLES TO
THE EPHESIANS, PHILIPPIANS, COLOSSIANS.
Three vols., 10/6 each ; *or set*, 18/- *net*.
Early Ideals of Righteousness : HEBREW, GREEK AND ROMAN.
By Prof. KENNETT, Mrs. ADAM, and Prof. GWATKIN. 3/- net.
Emmet (Rev. Cyril W.). ESCHATOLOGICAL QUESTION IN THE
GOSPELS, AND OTHER STUDIES IN RECENT NEW TESTAMENT CRITICISM. 6/- net.
Encyclopædia of Religion and Ethics. Edited by Dr.
HASTINGS. (*See page* 16.)
Eras of the Christian Church. *Complete in Ten Volumes—*

The Ecumenical Councils	Du Bose (Prof. W. P.).	6/-
The Post-Apostolic Age	WATERMAN (Dr. L.).	6/-
The Age of the Renascence	DYKE (PAUL VAN).	6/-
The Age of the Great Western Schism	LOCKE (Dr. CLINTON).	6/-
The Age of the Crusades	LUDLOW (Dr. J. M.).	6/-
The Age of Hildebrand	VINCENT (Prof. M. R.).	6/-
The Anglican Reformation	CLARK (Prof. W. R.).	6/-
The Age of Charlemagne	WELLS (Prof. C. L.).	6/-
The Apostolic Age.	BARTLET (Prof. J. VERNON).	6/-
The Protestant Reformation	WALKER (Prof. W.).	6/-

Ewald (Heinrich). HEBREW SYNTAX. 8/6.
Expository Times. Edited by Dr. HASTINGS.
Monthly, 6d. ; Annual subscription, post free, 6/-.
Fairweather (Dr. Wm.). THE BACKGROUND OF THE GOSPELS.
Judaism in the Period between the Old and New Testaments. 8/- net.
——— ORIGEN AND GREEK PATRISTIC THEOLOGY. 3/-.
Falconer (Rev. J. W.). FROM APOSTLE TO PRIEST. A Study
of Early Church Organisation. 4/6.
Farnell (Dr. L. R.). GREECE AND BABYLON. A Comparative
Sketch of Mesopotamian, Anatolian, and Hellenic Religions. 7/6.
Ferries (Dr. George). THE GROWTH OF CHRISTIAN FAITH.
7/6 net.
Fisher (Prof. G. P.). HISTORY OF CHRISTIAN DOCTRINE.
(*International Theological Library.*) Second Edition, 12/-.
Fisher (Dr. R. H.). THE BEATITUDES. (*Short Course Series.*)
2/- net.
Forbes (Rev. J. T.). SOCRATES. 3/-.
Foreign Theological Library. Four Vols. for One Guinea net.
Detailed List on application.
Forrest (Dr. D. W.). THE CHRIST OF HISTORY AND OF EX-
PERIENCE. Sixth Edition, 6/-.
——— THE AUTHORITY OF CHRIST. Third Edition, 6/-.
Frame (Prof. J. E.). THESSALONIANS. (*International Critical
Commentary.*) 10/6.
Funcke (Otto). THE WORLD OF FAITH AND THE EVERYDAY
WORLD, as displayed in the Footsteps of Abraham. 7/6.
Garvie (Principal A. E.). THE RITSCHLIAN THEOLOGY. 2nd Ed.,9/-.
Geden (Prof. A. S.). OUTLINES OF INTRODUCTION TO THE
HEBREW BIBLE. With Fourteen Illustrations. 8/6 net.

Geere (H. Valentine). By Nile and Euphrates. A Record of Discovery and Adventure.   8/6 net.

Gem (Rev. S. H.). An Anglo-Saxon Abbot. Ælfric of Eynsham.   4/- net.

Gladden (Dr. Washington). The Christian Pastor and the Working Church. (*International Theological Library.*)   10/6.

Gloag (Dr. Paton J.). The Messianic Prophecies.   7/6.

—— Introduction to the Catholic Epistles.   10/6.

—— Introduction to the Synoptic Gospels.   7/6.

—— Exegetical Studies.   5/-.

Godet (Prof. F.). An Introduction to the New Testament.
I. The Epistles of St. Paul.   12/6 net.
II. The Gospel Collection, and St. Matthew's Gospel.   6/- net.

—— Commentary on St. Luke's Gospel, 2 vols., 12/- net; Commentary on St. John's Gospel, 3 vols., 18/- net; Commentary on Epistle to the Romans, 2 vols., 12/- net; Commentary on First Epistle to Corinthians, 2 vols., 12/- net.
*** Any Four Volumes at the original Subscription price of 21/- net.

—— Defence of the Christian Faith.   4/-.

Goebel (Siegfried). The Parables of Jesus.   6/- net.

Gordon (Prof. Alex. R.). The Early Traditions of Genesis.   6/- net.

Gould (Prof. E. P.). St. Mark. (*International Critical Commentary.*)   10/6.

Graham (David). The Grammar of Philosophy. A Study of Scientific Method.   7/6 net.

Gray (Prof. G. Buchanan). Numbers. (*International Critical Commentary.*)   12/-.

—— Isaiah, i.-xxvii. (*International Critical Commentary.*)   12/-.

Great Texts of the Bible, The. Edited by Dr. Hastings. Four Volumes published annually, 10/- per vol. Advance Subscription Terms, 6/- net per volume. Twelve Volumes ready :—Genesis to Numbers ; Deuteronomy to Esther ; Job to Psalm 30 ; Isaiah ; St. Mark ; St. John, 2 vols. ; Acts & Romans 1-8 ; Romans (completion) ; 1 Corinthians ; Ephesians to Colossians ; James to Jude. *Full Prospectus free*

Gregory (Prof. C. R.). The Canon and Text of the New Testament. (*International Theological Library.*)   12/-.

Grimm's Greek-English Lexicon of the New Testament. Translated, Revised, and Enlarged by Joseph H. Thayer, D.D.   Fourth Edition, Demy 4to, 36/-.

Guyot (Arnold, LL.D.). Creation; or, The Biblical Cosmogony in the Light of Modern Science. With Illustrations.   5/6.

Gwatkin (Prof. H. M.). The Knowledge of God and its Historical Development. Two vols.   Second Edition, 12/- net.

—— The Eye for Spiritual Things.   4/6 net.

Hagenbach (Dr. K. R.). History of Doctrines. 3 vols.   18/- net.

Halcombe (Rev. J. J.). What Think Ye of the Gospels?   3/6.

Hall (Dr. Newman). Divine Brotherhood.   3rd Edition, 4/-.

Hamilton (Dr. Thos.). Beyond the Stars; or, Heaven, its Inhabitants, Occupations, and Life.   Third Edition, 3/6.

Harper (Pres. W. R.). Amos and Hosea. (*International Critical Commentary.*)   12/-.

Harris (Prof. Samuel). God the Creator and Lord of All. Two vols.   16/-.

Hastie (Prof. Wm.). THEOLOGY OF THE REFORMED CHURCH IN ITS FUNDAMENTAL PRINCIPLES (*Croall Lectures*). **4/6** net.

———— OUTLINES OF PASTORAL THEOLOGY. For Young Ministers and Students. **1/6** net.

Hastings (Dr. James). Works Edited by.
See 'Great Texts of the Bible,' p. 6; 'Expository Times,' p. 5; 'Scholar as Preacher' Series, p. 12; and Dictionaries, p. 16.

Heard (Rev. J. B.). THE TRIPARTITE NATURE OF MAN. **6/-.**

———— OLD AND NEW THEOLOGY. A Constructive Critique. **6/-.**

———— ALEXANDRIAN AND CARTHAGINIAN THEOLOGY CONTRASTED. **6/-.**

Hefele (Bishop). A HISTORY OF THE COUNCILS OF THE CHURCH. Vol. I., to A.D. 325. Vol. II., A.D. 326 to 429. Vol. III., A.D. 431 to the close of the Council of Chalcedon, 451. Vol. IV., A.D. 451 to 680. Vol. V., A.D. 626 to 787. **12/-** each.

Henderson (Rev. George). THE BIBLE A REVELATION FROM GOD. **6d.** net.

Henderson (Rev. H. F.). THE RELIGIOUS CONTROVERSIES OF SCOTLAND. **4/6** net.

Herkless (Prof. John). FRANCIS AND DOMINIC. **3/-.**

Heron (Prof. James). A SHORT HISTORY OF PURITANISM. **1/-** net.

Hill (Dr. J. Hamlyn). ST. EPHRAEM THE SYRIAN. **7/6.**

———— THE EARLIEST LIFE OF CHRIST: BEING THE DIATESSARON OF TATIAN. A Popular Edition, with Introduction. **3/-** net.

Hodgson (Geraldine, B.A.). PRIMITIVE CHRISTIAN EDUCATION. **4/6** net.

Hodgson (Principal J. M.). THEOLOGIA PECTORIS: Outlines of Religious Faith and Doctrine. **3/6.**

Hogg (Prof. A. G.). CHRIST'S MESSAGE OF THE KINGDOM. Paper covers, **1/6** net; cloth, **2/-** net.

Holborn (Rev. Alfred). THE PENTATEUCH IN THE LIGHT OF TO-DAY. Second Edition, **2/-** net.

Holborn (I. B. Stoughton). THE ARCHITECTURES OF THE RELIGIONS OF EUROPE. **6/-** net.

Hudson (Prof. W. H.). ROUSSEAU, AND NATURALISM IN LIFE AND THOUGHT. **3/-.**

Hügel (Baron F. von). ETERNAL LIFE. A Study of its Implications and Applications. **8/-** net.

Hutton (Archdeacon W. H.). A DISCIPLE'S RELIGION. **4/6** net.

Inge (Dean W. R.). FAITH AND KNOWLEDGE. **4/6** net.

Innes (Arthur D.). CRANMER AND THE ENGLISH REFORMATION. **3/-.**

Innes (A. Taylor, LL.D.). THE TRIAL OF JESUS CHRIST. In its Legal Aspect. Second Edition, **2/6.**

International Critical Commentary on the Old and New Testaments.

Genesis	SKINNER (Principal JOHN). **12/6**
Numbers	GRAY (Prof. G. BUCHANAN). **12/-**
Deuteronomy	DRIVER (Prof. S. R.). **12/-**
Judges	MOORE (Prof. G. F.). **12/-**
1 and 2 Samuel . . .	SMITH (Prof. H. P.). **12/-**
1 and 2 Chronicles . . .	CURTIS (Prof E. L.). **12/-**
Esther	PATON (Prof. L. B.). **10/6**
Psalms	BRIGGS (Prof. C. A.).
	2 vols., each **10/6**
Proverbs	TOY (Prof. C. H.). **12/-**
Ecclesiastes	BARTON (Prof. G. A.). **8/6**
Isaiah i.–xxvii. . . .	GRAY (Prof. G. BUCHANAN). **12/-**
Amos and Hosea . . .	HARPER (Dr. W. R.). **12/-**

International Critical Commentary—*continued.*

Haggai, Zechariah, Malachi, and Jonah — Mitchell (Prof. H. G.), Smith (Prof. J. M. P.), and Bewer (Prof. J. A.). **12/-**

Micah, Zephaniah, Nahum, Habakkuk, Obadiah, and Joel — Smith (Prof. J. M. P.), Ward (Prof. W. H.), and Bewer (Prof. J. A.). **12/6**

St. Matthew — Allen (Rev. W. C.). **12/-**
St. Mark — Gould (Prof. E. P.). **10/6**
St. Luke — Plummer (Dr. A.). **12/-**
Romans — Sanday (Prof. W.), and Headlam (Prin. A. C.). **12/-**
1 Corinthians — Robertson (Rt. Rev. Arch.) and Plummer (Dr. A.). **12/-**
Ephesians and Colossians — Abbott (Prof. T. K.). **10/6**
Philippians and Philemon — Vincent (Prof. M. R.). **8/6**
Thessalonians — Frame (Prof. J. E.). **10/6**
St. Peter and St. Jude — Bigg (Prof. C.). **10/6**
The Johannine Epistles — Brooke (Rev. A. E.). **10/6**

International Theological Library.

The Doctrine of the Person of Jesus Christ — By Prof. H. R. Mackintosh. **10/6**
An Introduction to the Literature of the Old Testament. — By Prof. S. R. Driver. **12/-**
Christian Ethics — By Dr. Newman Smyth. **10/6**
Theology of the Old Testament — By Prof. A. B. Davidson. **12/-**
History of the Reformation — By Principal T. M. Lindsay. 2 vols., **10/6** each.
An Introduction to the Literature of the New Testament — By Prof. James Moffatt. **12/-**
Old Testament History — By Prof. H. P. Smith. **12/-**
Apologetics — By Prof. A. B. Bruce. **10/6**
The Christian Doctrine of God — By Prof. W. N. Clarke. **10/6**
History of Christian Doctrine — By Prof. G. P. Fisher. **12/-**
The Greek and Eastern Churches — By Principal W. F. Adeney. **12/-**
Christian Institutions — By Prof. A. V. G. Allen. **12/-**
The Apostolic Age — By Prof. A. C. McGiffert. **12/-**
The Christian Pastor — By Dr. W. Gladden. **10/6**
Canon and Text of the New Testament — By Prof. C. R. Gregory. **12/-**
Theology of the New Testament — By Prof. G. B. Stevens. **12/-**
Christian Doctrine of Salvation — By Prof. G. B. Stevens. **12/-**
The Ancient Catholic Church — By Principal R. Rainy. **12/-**

Iverach (Principal James). Descartes, Spinoza, and the New Philosophy. **3/-.**

Janet (Paul). Final Causes. Second Edition, **12/-.**
—— The Theory of Morals. **10/6.**

Johns (Canon C. H. W.). The Oldest Code of Laws in the World. The Code of Laws promulgated by Hammurabi, King of Babylon, B.C. 2285-2242. **1/6** net.
—— Babylonian and Assyrian Laws, Contracts, and Letters **12/-** net.

Johnstone (P. De Lacy). Muhammad and his Power. **3/-.**

Jordan (Prof. W. G.). Biblical Criticism and Modern Thought; or, The Old Testament Documents in the Life of To-day. **7/6** net.
—— The Song and the Soil. (*Short Course Series.*) **2/** net.

Kaftan (Prof. Julius, D.D.). The Truth of the Christian Religion. *Authorised Translation.* 2 vols. **16/-** net.

Kant. Philosophy of Law. Trans. by Prof. Wm. Hastie. **5/-**

Keil (Prof.). PENTATEUCH, 3 vols. 8vo, **18/-** net; JOSHUA, JUDGES, AND RUTH, 8vo, **6/-** net; SAMUEL, 8vo, **6/-** net; KINGS, 8vo, **6/-** net; CHRONICLES, 8vo, **6/-** net; EZRA, NEHEMIAH, ESTHER, 8vo, **6/-** net; JEREMIAH, 2 vols. 8vo, **12/-** net; EZEKIEL, 2 vols. 8vo, **12/-** net; DANIEL, 8vo, **6/-** net; MINOR PROPHETS, 2 vols. 8vo, **12/-** net; INTRODUCTION TO THE CANONICAL SCRIPTURES OF THE OLD TESTAMENT, 2 vols. 8vo, **12/-** net; HANDBOOK OF BIBLICAL ARCHÆOLOGY, 2 vols. 8vo, **12/-** net.
** Any Four Volumes at the original Subscription price of 21/- net.

Kennedy (Dr. James). THE NOTE-LINE IN THE HEBREW SCRIPTURES. **4/6** net.

Kennett (Prof. R. H.), Adam (Mrs.), and Gwatkin (Prof. H. M.). EARLY IDEALS OF RIGHTEOUSNESS. **3/-** net.

Kilpatrick (Prof. T. B.). CHRISTIAN CHARACTER. **2/6.**

König (Dr. Ed.). THE EXILES' BOOK OF CONSOLATION (Deutero-Isaiah). **3/6.**

König (Dr. F. E.). THE RELIGIOUS HISTORY OF ISRAEL. **3/6.**

Krause (F. C. F.). THE IDEAL OF HUMANITY. **3/-.**

Krummacher (Dr. F. W.). DAVID, THE KING OF ISRAEL. Second Edition, **6/-.**

Kurtz (Prof.). HANDBOOK OF CHURCH HISTORY (from 1517). **7/6.**

—— HISTORY OF THE OLD COVENANT. Three vols. **18/-** net.

Ladd (Prof. G. T.). THE DOCTRINE OF SACRED SCRIPTURE. Two vols., 1600 pp. **24/-.**

Laidlaw (Prof. John). THE BIBLE DOCTRINE OF MAN. **7/6.**

Lambert (Dr. J. C.). THE SACRAMENTS IN THE NEW TESTAMENT. **10/6.**

Lane (Laura M.). LIFE OF ALEXANDER VINET. **7/6.**

Lange (Prof. John P.). THE LIFE OF OUR LORD JESUS CHRIST. Edited by MARCUS DODS, D.D. 2nd Edition, in 4 vols., price **28/-** net.

—— COMMENTARY ON THE OLD AND NEW TESTAMENTS. Edited by PHILIP SCHAFF, D.D. OLD TESTAMENT, 14 vols.; NEW TESTAMENT, 10 vols.; APOCRYPHA, 1 vol. **15/-** net each.

—— ST. MATTHEW AND ST. MARK, 3 vols., **18/-** net; ST. LUKE, 2 vols. **12/-** net; ST. JOHN, 2 vols. **12/-** net. Any Four Volumes at the original Subscription price of 21/- net.

Law (Prof. Robert). THE TESTS OF LIFE. A Study of the First Epistle of St. John. Second Edition, **7/6** net.

Le Camus (E., Bishop of La Rochelle). THE CHILDREN OF NAZARETH. Fcap. 4to. **2/6** net.

Lechler (Prof. G. V.). THE APOSTOLIC AND POST-APOSTOLIC TIMES. Their Diversity and Unity in Life and Doctrine. 2 vols. **16/-.**

Leckie (Rev. Joseph H.). AUTHORITY IN RELIGION. **5/-.**

Lehmann (Pastor). SCENES FROM THE LIFE OF JESUS. **3/6.**

Lendrum (Rev. R. A.). AN OUTLINE OF CHRISTIAN TRUTH. **6d.** net.

Lewis (Rev. George). THE PHILOCALIA OF ORIGEN. **7/6** net.

Lewis (Dr. Tayler). THE SIX DAYS OF CREATION. **7/6.**

Lilley (Dr. J. P.). THE LORD'S SUPPER: Its Origin, Nature, and Use. **5/-.**

Lillie (Arthur). BUDDHA AND BUDDHISM. **3/-.**

Lindsay (Principal Thos. M.). HISTORY OF THE REFORMATION. (*International Theological Library.*) 2 vols. **10/6** each.

—— LUTHER AND THE GERMAN REFORMATION. **3/-.**

Locke (Dr. Clinton). THE AGE OF THE GREAT WESTERN SCHISM. (*Eras of Church History.*) **6/-.**

Lotze (Hermann). MICROCOSMUS: An Essay concerning Man and his relation to the World. 2 vols. (1450 pp.). 24/-.

Ludlow (Dr. J. M.). THE AGE OF THE CRUSADES. (*Eras of Church History.*) 6/-.

Luthardt (Prof.). COMMENTARY ON ST. JOHN'S GOSPEL. 3 vols. 18/- net.

—— HISTORY OF CHRISTIAN ETHICS. 6/- net.

—— THE FUNDAMENTAL TRUTHS OF CHRISTIANITY. 7th Ed. 6/-.

McCosh (Principal James, of Princeton), Life of. 9/-.

MacCulloch (Canon John A.). THE RELIGION OF THE ANCIENT CELTS. 10/- net.

McFadyen (Prof. J. E.). A CRY FOR JUSTICE. (*Short Course Series.*) 2/- net.

—— THE HISTORICAL NARRATIVE OF THE OLD TESTAMENT. 6d. net.

McGiffert (Prof. A. C.). HISTORY OF CHRISTIANITY IN THE APOSTOLIC AGE. (*International Theological Library.*) 12/-.

—— THE APOSTLES' CREED. 4/- net.

Macgregor (Rev. G. H. C.). SO GREAT SALVATION. 1/-.

Macgregor (Dr. Wm. M.). JESUS CHRIST THE SON OF GOD. Sermons and Interpretations. 4/6 net.

—— SOME OF GOD'S MINISTRIES. 4/6 net.

M'Hardy (Dr. George). SAVONAROLA. 3/-.

—— THE HIGHER POWERS OF THE SOUL. (*Short Course Series.*) 2/- net.

Macpherson (Rev. John). COMMENTARY ON EPHESIANS. 10/6.

M'Intosh (Rev. Hugh). IS CHRIST INFALLIBLE AND THE BIBLE TRUE? Third Edition, 6/- net.

Mackintosh (Prof. H. R.). THE DOCTRINE OF THE PERSON OF JESUS CHRIST. (*International Theological Library.*) Second Ed., 10/6.

Mackintosh (Prof. Robert). HEGEL AND HEGELIANISM. 3/-.

M'Laren (Rev. Wm. D.). OUR GROWING CREED. 9/- net.

Marjoribanks (Rev. Thos.). THE SEVENFOLD 'I AM.' (*Short Course Series.*) 2/- net.

Martensen (Bishop). CHRISTIAN DOGMATICS. 6/- net.

— CHRISTIAN ETHICS. (GENERAL — INDIVIDUAL — SOCIAL.) Three vols. 6/- net each.

Matheson (Geo., D.D.). GROWTH OF THE SPIRIT OF CHRISTIANITY from the First Century to the Dawn of the Lutheran Era. Two vols. 21s.

Meyer (Dr.). CRITICAL AND EXEGETICAL COMMENTARY ON THE NEW TESTAMENT. Twenty vols. 8vo. *Subscription price, £5, 5/- net; selection of Four Volumes at Subscription price of 21/-; Non-Subscription price,* 10/6 each volume.

ST. MATTHEW, 2 vols.; MARK AND LUKE, 2 vols.; ST. JOHN, 2 vols.; ACTS, 2 vols.; ROMANS, 2 vols.; CORINTHIANS, 2 vols.; GALATIANS, one vol.; EPHESIANS AND PHILEMON, one vol.; PHILIPPIANS AND COLOSSIANS, one vol.; THESSALONIANS (*Dr. Lünemann*), one vol.; THE PASTORAL EPISTLES (*Dr. Huther*), one vol.; HEBREWS (*Dr. Lünemann*), one vol.; ST. JAMES AND ST. JOHN'S EPISTLES (*Huther*), one vol.; PETER AND JUDE (*Dr. Huther*), one vol.

Michie (Charles, M.A.). BIBLE WORDS AND PHRASES. 1/-.

Milligan (Prof. Wm.) and **Moulton (Dr. W. F.).** COMMENTARY ON THE GOSPEL OF ST. JOHN. 9/-.

Mitchell (Prof. H. G.), Smith (Prof. J. M. P.), and **Bewer** (Prof. J. A.). HAGGAI, ZECHARIAH, MALACHI, and JONAH. (*International Critical Commentary.*) 12/-.

Moffatt (Prof. James). INTRODUCTION TO THE LITERATURE OF THE NEW TESTAMENT. (*International Theological Library.*) 2nd Ed., 12/-.

Moore (**Prof. G. F.**). JUDGES. (*International Critical Commentary.*) Second Edition, 12/-.

Moulton (**Prof. James H.**). A GRAMMAR OF NEW TESTAMENT GREEK. Part I. The Prolegomena. Third Edition, 8/- net.

Moulton (**Dr. W. F.**) and **Geden** (**Prof. A. S.**). A CONCORDANCE TO THE GREEK TESTAMENT. Third Edition. Crown 4to, 26/- net and 31/6 net.

Murray (**Prof. J. Clark**). A HANDBOOK OF CHRISTIAN ETHICS. 6/- net.

Naville (**Ernest**). THE CHRIST. 4/6.

——— MODERN PHYSICS. 5/-.

Nicoll (**Sir W. Robertson**). THE INCARNATE SAVIOUR. 3/6.

Novalis. HYMNS AND THOUGHTS ON RELIGION. 4/-.

Oehler (**Prof.**). THEOLOGY OF THE OLD TESTAMENT. Two vols. 12/- net.

Oosterzee (**Dr. Van**). THE YEAR OF SALVATION. Two vols. 6/- each.

——— MOSES: A Biblical Study. 6/-.

Orelli (**Dr. C. von**). OLD TESTAMENT PROPHECY; COMMENTARY ON ISAIAH; JEREMIAH; THE TWELVE MINOR PROPHETS. 4 vols. Subscription price, 21s. net; separate vols., 6s. net each.

Origen, The Philocalia of. Translated by Rev. GEORGE LEWIS, M.A. 7/6 net.

Orr (**Prof. James, D.D.**). DAVID HUME, AND HIS INFLUENCE ON PHILOSOPHY AND THEOLOGY. 3/-.

Owen (**Dr. John**). WORKS. *Best and only Complete Edition.* Edited by Rev. Dr. GOOLD. Twenty-four vols. 8vo. Subscription price, £4, 4/-.
The '*Hebrews*' may be had separately, in seven vols., £1, 5/- net.

Palestine, Map of. Edited by J. G. BARTHOLOMEW, F.R.G.S., and Principal G. A. SMITH, LL.D. With complete Index. Scale—4 Miles to an Inch. In cloth case, 10/6; mounted on rollers, varnished, 15/-.

Paton (**Prof. L. B., Ph.D.**). THE BOOK OF ESTHER. (*International Critical Commentary.*) 10/6.

Patrick (**Principal W.**). JAMES, THE LORD'S BROTHER. 6/- net.

Paulin (**George**). NO STRUGGLE FOR EXISTENCE, NO NATURAL SELECTION. 5/- net.

Plummer (**Dr. Alfred**). ST. LUKE. (*International Critical Commentary.*) Fourth Edition, 12/-.

——— ENGLISH CHURCH HISTORY. Three volumes (1509–1575, 1575–1649, and 1649–1702). 3/- net each.

Popular Commentary on the New Testament. Edited by Dr. PHILIP SCHAFF. With Illustrations and Maps. Vol. I. THE SYNOPTICAL GOSPELS. Vol. II. ST. JOHN'S GOSPEL AND THE ACTS OF THE APOSTLES. Vol. III. ROMANS TO PHILEMON. In three vols. imperial 8vo. 12/6 each.

Primers for Teachers and Senior Bible Class Students. Edited by Rev. GEORGE HENDERSON, B.D. First three ready. 6d. net each. *See Primers by* HENDERSON (G.), LENDRUM (R.A.), *and* McFADYEN (J. E.).

Profeit (**Rev. W.**). THE CREATION OF MATTER; or, Material Elements, Evolution, and Creation. 2/- net.

Pünjer (**Bernhard**). HISTORY OF THE CHRISTIAN PHILOSOPHY OF RELIGION FROM THE REFORMATION TO KANT. 16/-.

Purves (**Dr. David**). THE LIFE EVERLASTING. 4/- net.

Rainy (**Principal R.**). DELIVERY AND DEVELOPMENT OF CHRISTIAN DOCTRINE. 10/6.

——— THE ANCIENT CATHOLIC CHURCH. (*International Theological Library.*) 12/-.

Rashdall (Rev. Hastings). CHRISTUS IN ECCLESIA.   4/6 net.

Reid (Rev. John). JESUS AND NICODEMUS. A Study in
Spiritual Life.   4/6 net.

Reusch (Prof.). NATURE AND THE BIBLE : Lectures on the Mosaic
History of Creation in relation to Natural Science.   Two vols.   21/-.

Reuss (Professor). HISTORY OF THE SACRED SCRIPTURES OF THE
NEW TESTAMENT.   640 pp.   15/-.

Richard (Dr. Timothy). THE NEW TESTAMENT OF HIGHER
BUDDHISM.   6/- net.

Riehm (Dr. E.) MESSIANIC PROPHECY.   Second Edition, 7/6.

Ritchie (Prof. D. G.). PLATO.   3/-.

Ritschl (Dr. Albrecht). THE CHRISTIAN DOCTRINE OF JUSTIFI-
CATION AND RECONCILIATION.   Second Edition, 14/-.

Ritter (Carl). COMPARATIVE GEOGRAPHY OF PALESTINE. 4 vols., 21/-.

Robertson (Rt. Rev. Archibald) and **Plummer (Dr.**
Alfred).   I. CORINTHIANS.   (*International Critical Commentary.*)   12/-.

Robinson (Prof. H. W.). THE CHRISTIAN DOCTRINE OF MAN.
                                                       6/- net.

Ross (C.). OUR FATHER'S KINGDOM ; or, The Lord's Prayer.   2/6.

Rothe (Prof.) SERMONS FOR THE CHRISTIAN YEAR.   4/6.

Royce (Prof. Josiah). THE SOURCES OF RELIGIOUS INSIGHT.
                                                       4/6 net.

Rutherfurd (Rev. John). ST. PAUL'S EPISTLES TO COLOSSÆ
AND LAODICEA.   6/- net.

Saisset. MANUAL OF MODERN PANTHEISM.   Two vols.   10/6.

Salmond (Princ. S. D. F.). THE CHRISTIAN DOCTRINE OF
IMMORTALITY.   Fifth Edition, 9/-.

———— THE SHORTER CATECHISM.   1/6.

———— *See Bible Class Primers, p.* 15.

Sanday (Prof. Wm.) and **Headlam (Princ. A. C.).** ROMANS.
(*International Critical Commentary.*)   Fifth Edition, 12/-.

Sanday (Prof. Wm.). OUTLINES OF THE LIFE OF CHRIST.
                                         Second Edition, 5/- net.

Sarolea (Dr. Charles). NEWMAN AND HIS INFLUENCE ON
RELIGIOUS LIFE AND THOUGHT.   3/-.

Sayce (Prof. A. H.). THE RELIGIONS OF ANCIENT EGYPT AND
BABYLONIA.   8/- net.

Schaff (Prof.). HISTORY OF THE CHRISTIAN CHURCH.   Six
'Divisions,' in 2 vols. each.
  1. APOSTOLIC CHRISTIANITY, A.D. 1–100, 2 vols. 21/-.   2. ANTE-NICENE,
  A.D. 100–325, 2 vols., 21/-.   3. NICENE AND POST-NICENE, A.D. 325–600,
  2 vols., 21/-.   4. MEDIÆVAL, A.D. 590–1073, 2 vols., 21/-.   5. THE SWISS
  REFORMATION, 2 vols., 21/-.   6. THE GERMAN REFORMATION, 2 vols., 21/-.

Scholar as Preacher Series. Edited by Dr. JAMES
HASTINGS.   Eleven volumes ready.   4/6 net each.
  See works by CLIFFORD (J.), COOKE (G. A.), DUDDEN (F. H.), GWATKIN
  (H. M.), HUTTON (W. H.), INGE (W. R.), MACGREGOR (W. M.), RASHDALL
  (H.), WOODS (H. C.), and ZAHN (TH.).

Schubert (Prof. H. Von). THE GOSPEL OF ST. PETER. Synoptical
Tables.   With Translation and Critical Apparatus.   1/6 net.

Schultz (Hermann). OLD TESTAMENT THEOLOGY.   Two vols.
                                                       18/- net.

Schürer (Prof. E.). HISTORY OF THE JEWISH PEOPLE.   Five vols.
Subscription price, 26/3 net.   Index in separate volume, 2/6 net.

Schwartzkopff (Dr. P.). THE PROPHECIES OF JESUS CHRIST. 5/-.

Scott (Prof. Ernest F.). THE FOURTH GOSPEL : Its Purpose
and Theology.   Second Edition, 6/- net.

Scott (Prof. Ernest F.). THE KINGDOM AND THE MESSIAH.
6/- net.
Scott (Dr. Robert). THE PAULINE EPISTLES. 6/- net.
Seaver (Rev. R. W.). TO CHRIST THROUGH CRITICISM. Post
8vo. 3/6 net.
Shaw (Dr. R. D.). THE PAULINE EPISTLES. Third Edition, 8/- net.
Short Course Series. Edited by Rev. JOHN ADAMS, B.D.
9 vols. ready, price 2/- net each. *Full Prospectus free.*
See Works by ADAMS (J.), FISHER (R. H.), JORDAN (W. G.), MARJORI-
BANKS (T.), McFADYEN (J. E.), M'HARDY (G.), STALKER (J.), and WHITE-
LAW (T.).
Sime (James). WILLIAM HERSCHEL AND HIS WORK. 3/-.
Simon (Prof. D. W.). RECONCILIATION BY INCARNATION. 7/6.
Skinner (Principal John). GENESIS. (*International Critical
Commentary.*) 12/6.
Smeaton (Oliphant). THE MEDICI AND THE ITALIAN RENAIS-
SANCE. 3/-.
Smith (Prof. H. P.). I. AND II. SAMUEL. (*International Critical
Commentary.*) 12/-.
—— OLD TESTAMENT HISTORY. (*International Theological Library.*) 12/-.
Smith (Prof. J. M. P.), Ward (Prof. W. H.), and **Bewer**
(**Prof. J. A.**). MICAH, ZEPHANIAH, NAHUM, HABAKKUK, OBADIAH, and
JOEL. (*International Critical Commentary.*) 12/6.
Smith (Prof. Thos.). MEDIÆVAL MISSIONS. 4/6.
—— EUCLID: HIS LIFE AND SYSTEM. 3/-.
Smyth (John, D.Ph.). TRUTH AND REALITY. 4/-.
Smyth (Dr. Newman). CHRISTIAN ETHICS. (*International Theo-
logical Library.*) Third Edition, 10/6.
Snell (F. J., M.A.). WESLEY AND METHODISM. 3/-.
Stahlin (Leonh.). KANT, LOTZE, AND RITSCHL. 9/-.
Stalker (Prof. James). LIFE OF JESUS CHRIST.
Large Type Edition, 3/6 ; Bible Class Handbook Edition, 1/6.
—— LIFE OF ST. PAUL. 3/6 and 1/6.
—— THE PSALM OF PSALMS. (*Short Course Series.*) 2/- net.
Stead (F. H.). THE KINGDOM OF GOD. 1/6.
Stevens (Prof. G. B.). THE THEOLOGY OF THE NEW TESTAMENT.
(*International Theological Library.*) 12/-.
—— THE CHRISTIAN DOCTRINE OF SALVATION. (*International
Theological Library.*) 12/-.
Stier (Dr. Rudolph). ON THE WORDS OF THE LORD JESUS.
Eight vols., Subscription price £2, 2/- net ; separate volumes, price 6/- net.
THE WORDS OF THE RISEN SAVIOUR, AND COMMENTARY ON THE EPISTLE OF
ST. JAMES, 6/- net. THE WORDS OF THE APOSTLES EXPOUNDED, 6/- net.
Stirling (Dr. J. Hutchison). PHILOSOPHY AND THEOLOGY. 9/-.
—— DARWINIANISM: Workmen and Work. 10/6.
—— WHAT *IS* THOUGHT? 10/6.
Stone (Principal D.) and **Simpson (Rev. D. C.).** COM-
MUNION WITH GOD. 4/- net.
Strachan (Rev. James). HEBREW IDEALS FROM THE STORY OF
THE PATRIARCHS. Part I., 2/-. Part II., 2/-. Two Parts bound in One
Volume, 3/- net.
Strahan (Rev. James). THE BOOK OF JOB INTERPRETED.
7/6 net.
Taylor (Rev. R. O. P.). THE ATHANASIAN CREED IN THE
TWENTIETH CENTURY. 4/- net.
Thomson (Prof. J. Arthur). THE BIBLE OF NATURE. 4/6 net.

Thorburn (Dr. Thos. J.). JESUS THE CHRIST. Historical or
Mythical ? 6/– net.

Thumb (Prof. Albert). HANDBOOK OF THE MODERN GREEK
VERNACULAR. 12/– net.

Tophel (Pastor G.). THE WORK OF THE HOLY SPIRIT. 2/6.

Toy (Prof. C. H.). PROVERBS. (*International Critical Commentary.*) 12/–.

Troup (Rev. G. E.). WORDS TO YOUNG CHRISTIANS : Being
Addresses to Young Communicants. 4/6.

Ullmann (Dr. Carl). THE SINLESSNESS OF JESUS. 5/–.

Vincent (Prof. M. R.). THE AGE OF HILDEBRAND. (*Eras of
Church History.*) 6/–.

—— PHILIPPIANS AND PHILEMON. (*International Critical Commentary.*) 8/6.

Walker (Prof. Dawson). THE GIFT OF TONGUES. 4/6 net.

Walker (Dr. James). ESSAYS, PAPERS, AND SERMONS. 6/–.

—— THEOLOGY AND THEOLOGIANS OF SCOTLAND. Second Edition, 3/6.

Walker (Prof. W.). THE PROTESTANT REFORMATION. (*Eras
of Church History.*) 6/–.

Walker (Rev. W. L.). THE SPIRIT AND THE INCARNATION.
Third Edition, 9/

—— THE CROSS AND THE KINGDOM. Second Edition, 9/–.

—— CHRISTIAN THEISM AND A SPIRITUAL MONISM. Second Ed., 9/–.

—— THE TEACHING OF CHRIST IN ITS PRESENT APPEAL.
Second Edition, 2/6 net.

—— THE GOSPEL OF RECONCILIATION. 5/–.

—— WHAT ABOUT THE NEW THEOLOGY ? Second Edition, 2/6 net.

Warfield (Prof. B. B.). THE RIGHT OF SYSTEMATIC THEOLOGY.
2/–.

Waterman (Dr. L.). THE POST-APOSTOLIC AGE. (*Eras of Church
History.*) 6/–.

Watt (W. A., D.Ph.). A STUDY OF SOCIAL MORALITY. 6/–.

Weiss (Prof. B.). BIBLICAL THEOLOGY OF NEW TESTAMENT.
Two vols. 12/– net.

—— LIFE OF CHRIST. Three vols. 18/– net.

Welch (Dr. A. C.). ANSELM AND HIS WORK. 3/–.

—— THE RELIGION OF ISRAEL UNDER THE KINGDOM. 7/6 net.

Wells (Prof. C. L.). THE AGE OF CHARLEMAGNE. (*Eras of the
Christian Church.*) 6/–.

Wendt (Prof. H. H.). THE TEACHING OF JESUS. Two vols. 21/–.

—— THE GOSPEL ACCORDING TO ST. JOHN. 7/6.

Wenley (Prof. R. M.). CONTEMPORARY THEOLOGY AND THEISM.
4/6.

—— KANT AND HIS PHILOSOPHICAL REVOLUTION. 3/–.

Whitelaw (Dr. Thos.). JEHOVAH-JESUS. (*Short Course Series.*)
2/– net.

Wilson (Dr. John). HOW GOD HAS SPOKEN. 5/– net.

Woods (Dr. H. G.). AT THE TEMPLE CHURCH. 4/6 net.

Woods (Rev. F. H.). THE HOPE OF ISRAEL. 3/6.

Workman (Prof. G. C.). THE TEXT OF JEREMIAH. 9/–.

Worsley (Rev. F. W.). THE FOURTH GOSPEL AND THE SYNOP-
TISTS. 3/– net.

Zahn (Prof. Theodor). BREAD AND SALT FROM THE WORD
OF GOD. Sermons. 4/6 net.

—— AN INTRODUCTION TO THE NEW TESTAMENT. In three
volumes. 36/– net.

Handbooks for Bible Classes and Private Students.

Edited by Principal ALEXANDER WHYTE, LL.D., and
Rev. JOHN KELMAN, D.D.

COMMENTARIES—

Princ. MARCUS DODS. **Genesis.** 2s.; Dr. JAS. MACGREGOR. **Exodus.** 2 vols., 2s. each; Princ. G. C. M. DOUGLAS. **Joshua.** 1s. 6d. **Judges.** 1s. 3d.; Prof. J. G. MURPHY. **Chronicles.** 1s. 6d.; Rev. JAMES AITKEN. **Job.** 1s. 6d.; Princ. M. DODS. **Haggai, Zechariah, Malachi.** 2s.; Princ. G. C. M. DOUGLAS. **Obadiah to Zephaniah.** 1s. 6d.; Rev. E. E. ANDERSON. **St. Matthew.** 2s. 6d.; Princ. T. M. LINDSAY. **St. Mark.** 2s. 6d. **St. Luke.** Vol. I. 2s., Vol. II. 1s. 3d.; Dr. G. REITH. **St. John.** 2 vols., 2s. each; Princ. T. M. LINDSAY. **Acts.** 2 vols., 1s. 6d. each; Princ. D. BROWN. **Romans.** 2s.; Dr. JAS. MACGREGOR. **Galatians.** 1s. 6d.; Prof. J. S. CANDLISH. **Ephesians.** 1s. 6d.; Dr. S. R. MACPHAIL. **Colossians.** 1s. 6d.; Prof. A. B. DAVIDSON. **Hebrews.** 2s. 6d.; Dr. J. P. LILLEY. **The Pastoral Epistles.** 2s. 6d.

GENERAL SUBJECTS—

Prof. JAMES STALKER. **The Life of Christ.** 1s. 6d. **The Life of St. Paul.** 1s. 6d. (*Large-Type Editions,* 3s. 6d. *each*); Dr. ALEX. WHYTE. **The Shorter Catechism.** 2s. 6d.; Prof. J. S. CANDLISH. **The Christian Sacraments.** 1s. 6d. **The Christian Doctrine of God.** 1s. 6d. **The Work of the Holy Spirit.** 1s. 6d. **The Biblical Doctrine of Sin.** 1s. 6d.; Dr. N. L. WALKER. **Scottish Church History.** 1s. 6d.; Dr. GEO. SMITH. **History of Christian Missions.** 2s. 6d.; Dr. ARCH. HENDERSON. **Palestine: Its Historical Geography.** 2s. 6d.; Princ. T. M. LINDSAY. **The Reformation.** 2s.; Rev. JOHN MACPHERSON. **The Sum of Saving Knowledge.** 1s. 6d. **The Confession of Faith.** 2s. **Presbyterianism.** 1s. 6d.; Prof. BINNIE. **The Church.** 1s. 6d.; Prof. T. B. KILPATRICK. **Butler's Three Sermons on Human Nature.** 1s. 6d.; Dr. THOS. HAMILTON. **History of the Irish Presbyterian Church.** 2s.; Rev. WM. SCRYMGEOUR. **Lessons on the Life of Christ.** 2s. 6d.; A. TAYLOR INNES. **Church and State.** 3s.; Rev. J. FEATHER. **The Last of the Prophets—John the Baptist.** 2s.; Dr. WM. FAIRWEATHER. **From the Exile to the Advent.** 2s.; Prof. J. LAIDLAW. **Foundation Truths of Scripture as to Sin and Salvation.** 1s. 6d.; Dr. L. A. MUIRHEAD. **The Times of Christ.** *New Edition.* 2s.; Dr. J. P. LILLEY. **The Principles of Protestantism.** 2s. 6d.; Rev. JAS. STRACHAN. **Hebrew Ideals from the Story of the Patriarchs.** 2 vols., 2s. each; or bound together in one vol., 3s. net; Dr. D. M. ROSS. **The Teaching of Jesus.** 2s.; Prof. J. DICK FLEMING. **Israel's Golden Age.** 1s. 6d.; Rev. W. BEVERIDGE. **Makers of the Scottish Church.** 2s.

BIBLE CLASS PRIMERS.

Edited by Principal S. D. F. SALMOND, D.D.

Paper Covers, 6d. *each* (*by post,* 7d.); *Cloth Covers,* 8d. *each* (*by post,* 9d.).

The Making of Israel. Abraham. By Prof. C. A. SCOTT.; **Moses. The Truth of Christianity.** By Principal J. IVERACH; **The Mosaic Tabernacle. The Minor Prophets.** By Rev. J. ADAMS; **Joshua and the Conquest.** By Prof. CROSKERY; **The Period of the Judges.** By Prof. J. A. PATERSON; **The Kings of Judah.** By Prof. GIVEN; **The Kings of Israel.** By Rev. W. WALKER; **David.** By Rev. P. THOMSON; **Solomon.** By Rev. R. WINTERBOTHAM; **Elijah and Elisha.** By Prof. R. G. MACINTYRE; **History of Babylonia and Assyria. History of Egypt.** By Prof. R. G. MURISON; **Jeremiah. Outlines of Protestant Missions.** By Dr. J. ROBSON; **Ezekiel.** By Rev. W. HARVEY-JELLIE; **The Exile and the Restoration.** By Prof. A. B. DAVIDSON; **Eli, Samuel, and Saul. Our Christian Passover.** By Dr. C. A. SALMOND; **Historical Connection between the Old and New Testaments.** By Principal J. SKINNER; **The Parables of our Lord. Peter. Christ. The Sabbath. Shorter Catechism,** *Three Parts* (also bound in one volume, 1s. 6d.). By the EDITOR; **The Story of Jerusalem.** By Rev. H. CALLAN; **The Miracles of our Lord.** By Prof. J. LAIDLAW; **Our Lord's Illustrations. St. Paul's Illustrations.** By Rev. R. R. RESKER; **St. John. Paul.** By Dr. P. J. GLOAG; **History of the English Bible.** By Rev. B. THOMSON; **Historical Geography of Palestine.** By Dr. S. R. MACPHAIL; **Christian Character. Christian Conduct.** By Prof. T. B. KILPATRICK; **The Kingdom of God,** *Three Parts* (also bound in one volume, 1s. 6d.). By F. H. STEAD; **Outlines of Early Church History.** By Dr. H. W. SMITH; **History of the Reformation.** By Prof. WITHEROW; **The Free Church of Scotland.** By Dr. C. G. M'CRIE; **The Covenanters.** By Rev. J. BEVERIDGE.

Extra Vols.: **Bible Words and Phrases.** By Rev. C. MICHIE. 1s.; **The Seven Churches of Asia.** By Miss DEBORAH ALCOCK. 1s.

Date Due